LAST FLESH

LAST FLESH

LIFE IN THE TRANSHUMAN ERA

CHRISTOPHER DEWDNEY

HarperCollins*PublishersLtd*

http://www.harpercollins.com/canada

HarperCollins books may be purchased for educational, business, or
sales promotional use. For information please write: Special Markets
Department, HarperCollins Canada, 55 Avenue Road, Suite 2900,
Toronto, Ontario M5R 3L2.

An early version of "The Death of Fashion" appeared in *Shift*
magazine.

Epigraph copyright © David Malouf 1978. Reproduced by permission
of the author c/o Rogers, Coleridge & White Ltd., 20 Powis Mews,
London W11 1JN. Extract from *Axiomatic* by Greg Egan reprinted by
permission of Millennium Publishers. Extract from *Engines of Creation*
by Eric K. Drexler reprinted by permission of Doubleday, a division of
Bantam Doubleday Dell. Extract from *Infinite in All Directions* by
Freeman Dyson reprinted by permission of HarperCollins Publishers.
Extract from *Consciousness Explained* by Daniel C. Dennett reprinted by
permission of Little, Brown and Company. Extract from *Mind Children*
by Hans Moravec, copyright © 1988 by Hans Moravec, reprinted by
permission of Harvard University Press.

First edition

Canadian Cataloguing in Publication Data

Dewdney, Christopher, 1951–
Last flesh : life in the transhuman era

ISBN 0-00-638472-2

1. Technology and civilization — Forecasting. I. Title.
HM221.D49 1998   303.48'3   C97-932318-5

98 99 00 01 02 HC 10 9 8 7 6 5 4 3 2 1

Printed and bound in the United States

For my mother,
who loves ideas.

Contents

Our bodies are not final. We are moving, all of us, in our common humankind, through the forms we love so deeply in one another, to what our hands have already touched in love-making and our bodies strain for in each other's darkness. Slowly, and with pain, over centuries, we move an infinitesimal space towards it. We are creating the lineaments of some final man, for whose delight we have prepared a landscape, and who can only be as god.

— *An Imaginary Life*, David Malouf

Introduction

The mathematician John von Neumann once said that "living organisms are ... highly improbable." Years earlier, at a quantum physics conference, an anonymous physicist described life as "a disease of matter." These observations are not only off-the-cuff, but chillingly objective. Derived from decades of consideration, they contain special insights into the enigma of living matter. They give us an alien's-eye view of life comparable to the strange and miraculous reality of life itself.

Life on earth has undergone two major metamorphoses: the first complex molecules that linked themselves together into self-reproducing units — and the emergence of human consciousness. Language was intimately connected to the development of consciousness, and it was, as Marshall McLuhan pointed out, the font of all subsequent technology. The acquisition of consciousness and language still overshadows any subsequent technological gains we have made, but all that is about to change.

We are on the verge of the next stage in life's evolution, the stage where, by human agency, life takes control of itself and guides its own destiny. Never before has human life been able to change itself, to reach into its own genetic structure and rearrange its molecular basis; now it can. Perhaps we are already in the last few generations of our embodiment as carbon-based life forms. What is relatively certain is that we are about to enter the transition period between the human and the posthuman eras — the transhuman age. The goal of transhumanism is to surpass our current biological limitations, be it our life span or the capabilities of our brain. This book is a personal look at this transitional period — its culture, media and technology.

On a planetary scale, most of us are already transhuman to some degree. We are the products of bioengineering. Our immune systems have been altered by decoy viruses injected via vaccines. We consume genetically altered food. We use mood-altering psychopharmaceuticals, from fermented grape juice to Prozac. More recently, our bodies have become sites for more than 250 types of artificial implants: synthetic heart valves, pacemakers, artificial hip and knee joints, synthetic arteries and eye lenses, not to mention those used in plastic surgery. Eventually neural implants will be used to augment our brains. Prostheses to restore the vision of blind patients have already been successfully implanted in human cortexes.

Biotechnology is modifying us as well. We are becoming organic symbionts, with baboon hearts, porcine livers, porcine skin grafts. The transplanting of human organs — particularly blood — is already routine. Hormone replacement therapy has become commonplace, and human trials with artificial organs, called "neo-organs," have already begun in France. This process will not stop; it will gather momentum, and shortly it will blossom into a panoply of discoveries, interventions and breakthroughs. There may be setbacks, as well as innovations of dubious safety, along the way, but the exponential effect of cumulative scientific data, doubling and then tripling, will accelerate the progress of research, resulting in a cascade of inventions.

There is also a new hubris sweeping through the scientific community. Visionary scientists are blueprinting the impossible, and their visions — human immortality, nanotechnology, populating the universe — no longer have the stigma of quackery they once had. Scientists such as Hans Moravec, K. Eric Drexler and Freeman J. Dyson have all published books claiming that it is simply a matter of time before their "impossible" schemes are realized. My book, in part, examines some of the personal, social and moral effects of this absolute transformation of what it means to be human.

The title of this book, *Last Flesh*, might more accurately be worded *Last Spontaneously Evolved Flesh*, because human DNA flesh will not disappear immediately. Our bodies will be transformed gradually. The sophistication of the human body argues strongly that it will be a viable, perhaps even preferable, alternative to silicon for many years to come. At the same time, we are also forging new social and political realities that may turn out to be more durable than our bodies.

Like many important human cultural undertakings, the transhuman era really has no specific beginning. In some respects it has been going on for centuries. I think that the defining event signalling its unequivocal arrival will be the first neural implant. After that, what might be referred to as the classic transhuman era will last anywhere from 50 to 500 years, depending on what happens next, and how fast it happens. There is no reason why humans, transhumans and posthumans cannot co-exist. Our worries that hostile super-intelligences will destroy us after we have created them is far-fetched. What *will* happen during the transhuman era is that mind and matter will blend. And, as the separate fields of bioengineering, artificial intelligence and robotics converge, the division between carbon-based life (as we currently know it) and artificial life will become less and less detectable.

The transhuman epoch will not be based as much on political, or even material, power as on the unprecedented expansion of human capabilities. Genetic engineering will soon create an equal partnership between us and DNA in determining our biological destiny. Neuroscience and artificial intelligence are about to give us the keys to our own consciousness and psychology. Computer-assisted literature and art, as well as sophisticated virtual realities, will give us a cultural richness hitherto undreamed of. In terms of engineering, our abilities will be unparalleled: nanotechnology, robotics and physics will produce astounding new advances. We are at the brink of being able to become whatever we want, where the distance between imagination and application will disappear. In *Last Flesh*, I explore the effects of some of these innovations.

In this book I also hope to show that our collective dreams reveal a destiny we will one day realize. Our visions, historically documented in our mythologies, are proof that we always knew our potential. Fundamental among these visions are the idea of immortality and the notion of an immaterial soul. Supernatural powers, telepathy and transmigration also seem strongly plausible to us. Our intuitive sense of these latent potentials of consciousness, which are nascent in our technology, has informed our religions and philosophies for thousands of years. Now the time may not be far off when we will see these aspirations become a tangible reality, rationally constructed by science out of the material realm we so long thought unbridgable to the immaterial.

But this book is not a technotopiast's rant. It lingers more on culture than on machines. It also looks at social issues — the personal and collective effects of technological upheaval. There are ominous trends that have the potential to stop our progress and reverse everything we have gained. For every new technology brings with it contradictory social effects — the potential to empower or subjugate those touched by it. Relatively cheap, mass-produced camcorders are a case in point. In the hands of ordinary citizens, they are a tool for democracy and can prevent the abuse of power, when, for example, they are used to document police brutality. Conversely, used for surveillance by governments or corporations, the same cameras become a threat to privacy. Privacy itself will become a zone of conflict: between digital libertarians — the "cipher punks" who strive to keep cryptography in the hands of citizens — and corporations and governments — the apparent enemies of electronic privacy.

The introduction of transhuman technologies will have profoundly revolutionary, perhaps politically destabilizing, effects on the new world order. Even now, as new technologies are being introduced, we are entering an ominous period of growing scientific illiteracy, an age of superstition and dangerous credulity. According to the American Booksellers Association, the sale of New Age books jumped from 5.6 million copies in 1992 to 9.7 million in 1995. A Gallup poll taken in 1995 reported that 25 percent of Americans believe in ghosts, 10 percent claimed to have seen ghosts and 10 percent said they have personally talked to the devil. A 1992 Roper poll revealed that 16 percent of Americans believe they've had some form of contact with beings from another realm. A 1996 Gallup survey found that 49 percent of Canadians believe that antibiotics would be effective against viral illnesses such as colds and the flu. The time is ripe for a new dark age. A disturbing irrationality is forming in the slipstreams of the new media.

It is important at this point in our history, when we are about to take our most momentous step, possibly leaving our DNA-based substrate behind, to prepare our psychology for the next phase. It may well transpire that, after the transhuman era, humans will cease to exist — at least as we currently know them. But consciousness will certainly not end. We are approaching a terrifying, intoxicating and possibly dangerous threshold, a border of awareness on whose other side is a mystery as imponderable as anything we have yet wondered about.

Chapter 1

MEDIA CULTURE

TECHNOLOGY, VIETNAM AND THE NEW WORLD ORDER

North American culture on the cusp of the millennium has been largely defined by economic and technological traumas. The war in Vietnam and the oil crisis of the early seventies defined their period, but the spectacle of a mass culture that has begun to cannibalize itself has become the dominant motif of the late twentieth century.

Culture is locked into a self-appropriative spiral that winds tighter and tighter. For that reason, not only has originality become a scarce resource in the vampiric economy of our exhausted media landscape, but it is mistrusted and pursued at the same time. Fashion and entertainment, borrowing heavily from their pasts, have become "recombinant" fields where yesterday's styles are appropriated and recombined — little is created, few original values are formed. Hollywood recycles old TV shows into new movies while new movies become next year's TV shows.

The Collapse of History

If our posthistoric era was signalled by the death of originality and the rise of recombinant culture, it also had another origin — America's defeat in Vietnam. The Vietnam War directly questioned faith in technology. The malaise spawned by the first brush with technological impotence has consequently saturated Western culture. The tragedy of Vietnam came at the same time as the cancellation of the Apollo space program. Furthermore, the convergence of the oil crisis and the recession of the early seventies marked America's first faltering, its first falling-back from the future.

The six Apollo moon missions, from 1969 to 1972, represented a high-water mark in wealth and technology for the Western military-industrial complex. The fact is that we as a species can no longer afford the fuel bills of the giant Saturn V moon rockets. Our current spate of military-industrial downsizing gives poignant irony to the term "postmodern." We are floundering in the void left by a discredited future we still vaguely believe in. Certainly America's victory in the Gulf War redeemed its honour, and bolstered faith in military technology, but it came too late to assuage the systemic disappointment that arose from both the closing of the interplanetary frontier and the beginning of economic uncertainty. The Gulf War was not enough to restart history.

The Once Future Era

From 1969 to 1972, the world had many of the basic components we have today — it had lasers, nuclear weapons, colour television and rock 'n' roll. But it also had manned moon missions, not just shuttle missions to space-platforms orbiting the planet's suburbs. Additionally, those four years were a cultural acme. The psychedelic revolution was well under way, with its proliferation of creativity, and a global liberalization sparked by student protests seemed to be imminent.

This liberalization was snagged by a spider in the ointment: Vietnam. The cold war had been labouring for two decades to produce a ritual war, and Vietnam was the progeny of détente's sinister paradigm. The Vietnam War (whose aerial bombardments must have been visible to the Apollo astronauts looking down at the night side of the Earth) was a synthesis of all the major cultural, geopolitical and technological components of the late twentieth century.

Target Acquisition

Vietnam was a confrontation between historical, Western civilization and the political products of Western media and ideology. Certainly there was irony in the conflict as two Western orthodoxies (Marxism and Democracy) slugged it out in an Asian jungle. But Vietnam was centrally a media war, waged on television. The TV audience saw that the Vietnam War was not just about nationalism or ideological combat; it was very much about what is called in military parlance "target acquisition." It was a guerrilla war waged in a complex tropical/visual environment that mimicked the tactility of television. Jungle war was, and is, television war. It is also camouflage war. Vietnam taught Americans that things are not what they seem. Just as the Americans themselves, two centuries earlier, during the War of Independence, had "played dirty" against numerically superior British forces (with their inflexible rules of engagement), so the Vietcong exploited Occidental logic on all levels.

For American soldiers, the war became a struggle to simply identify the enemy. The Vietcong were racially invisible against the background of "friendly" Vietnamese. They were also logistically invisible, with their shadowy divisions in the jungle. Because the Vietcong's identity was ideological, consisting of a belief that had no political engagement with what the Americans called a "policing" operation, the Vietcong's motivations were intangible.

At the same time, the Americans were highly identifiable, and thus vulnerable. This vulnerability led to individual American soldiers creating their own criteria for enemy identification, with the concomitant slaughter of many innocents. Certainly, the determination and tenacity of the Vietcong was formidable, and they were most certainly ruthless. But because the ideology that ostensibly drove the Vietcong was more pragmatic than that of the Americans, there was a paradoxical lack of personal malice in the Vietcongs' warfare — though it was no less deadly.

Media War

American soldiers, coming from a media-saturated culture, were confronted with an enemy that was both alien to American culture and yet deeply embedded in America's dominant medium: television. This is what made the battle scenes such compelling TV. The activities of the Vietcong became the content of a provisional media whose intelligence gathering was both military and journalistic, just as it was in the Gulf War. (Though the military exerted much more control over civilian journalism during the Gulf War than in the Vietnam War.)

Logistically, the Vietnam War was absurd. For the Americans, it wove inanity with mortality. Nothing was discrete; everything was interconnected. There were no definite zones, and there was no defensible position. (The DMZ was an idea, a superimposed and unsuccessful Cartesian fantasy.) There was only the technology of war and the technology of telecommunication.

In Vietnam, the human organism, vulnerable and savage, was in a jungle on all levels: an amoral ideological jungle, a visual jungle, and a microbial jungle where the margins between predator and parasite blurred, where leeches in rice paddies drew as much blood as did enemy sniper fire. It was a war of sappers, of individual initiative, a phantasmagoria of cultural colonialism and pain. And all of this fed the ghost empire of Western media, so apparently solid, so ever-present, and yet so discorporate. The immediacy of the conflict made it seem to the television viewer back in America as if Vietnam were a geographic extension of Hawaii, or perhaps a part of California that was held by hostile forces.

Vietnam was also a confrontation between the twentieth century and primitive culture, between American soldiers newly tribalized by electronic media, and indigenous jungle peoples operating under the imperative of a nineteenth-century political ideology. (The American campaign in Vietnam was a casualty of a technological Maginot Syndrome — namely, that a new technology is sometimes vulnerable to primitive technologies. A later example of this was an incident that occurred during the Iran hostage crisis in 1979. Just before the crisis, sensitive intelligence documents in the American embassy were shredded. Iranian rug weavers, however, painstakingly reconstructed the shredded CIA documents. Exacting and plentiful hand labour — a medieval technology — overcame high-tech CIA shredders, much to the eventual embarrassment of the CIA.) Vietnam was infrared night scopes and jellied gasoline versus bamboo spikes poisoned with feces, carpet-bombing versus underground tunnels. It was the interface of bodies with machines, and the disastrous intersection of flesh with metal moving at high velocities. It was about the vulnerability of flesh, the adaptability of flesh versus the irreducible inflexibility of metal.

Media Containment and the Speed of War

Vietnam was also the second contained war, the second major war, after the Korean War, that didn't escalate into a world conflict. It was a demonstration of limited-theatre warfare, where modern superpower status didn't ensure victory. It was also the beginning of the end of superpowers, not by direct defeat, but because any conflict subjected to the exaggerative power of the media becomes, by default, a global spectacle that we all participate in, if only as media bystanders.

During the Vietnam conflict, the speed of media journalism caught up with the speed of war and was able to outflank the velocity of tactical surprise. Consequently, any conflict now takes place within the highly defined perimeters that the media set for it. A war can escalate only as quickly as it can outpace media coverage. Whereas the Falklands War was slower than its media coverage, the Gulf War was arguably as fast as its media coverage, at least in the first few days.

The Falklands War was almost a non-event as far as the news media were concerned. After the British fleet (an anachronism of pre-industrial technology) steamed out of British ports, the news media almost let the story die in the week that it took the fleet to get to the Falkland Islands. Naval convoys were too slow for TV. Only when action actually began did the media pick up the story in earnest. (There was a singular event in the middle of the conflict that revealed the mutual dependency of civilian and military telecommunications. The Exocet missile that destroyed HMS *Sheffield* got through the ship's electronic defences because they had been temporarily lowered to allow the commander to phone his family in England.)

The Gulf War, on the other hand, marked the beginning of a partial redemption of technology. It *was* fast enough to be media-worthy. The attention of the world as a single television audience was tangible throughout the conflict. War journalism had come a long way since the Second World War, when film footage took days to transport and process. The Gulf War was not only the first completely live war, but also the first war in which politicians looked to broadcast television in order to see how their military campaign was unfolding.

The Vietnam War was not just a media war; it was also about technological limitations, and the false sense of omniscience that military and electronic communications induced in U.S. soldiers. Personal danger became paradoxical: the American soldier was dropped into an alien environment and was offered the illusion that his presence was contingent or temporary. The war was a metaphor for personal mortality as a contradictory tragedy in the midst of redemptive technologies. The individual soldier existed in two, incommensurable realms — the universal grid of navigation latitudes and the private, mortal and intimate jungle. Thus, a precise airstrike could be called in, but, at the same time, an infection from a poisoned trail spike could prove to be fatal.

Ultimately, Vietnam was a sensorium of textures and sub-stances, of leaves and steel, of morphine and blood, of music and screams. This was a war fought at the height of the psychedelic era. At the same time as a LERP was leaving on a night mission from a base in Vietnam, an astronaut was teeing off on the moon, and all of this was viewed on a colour-television screen in the living room of an eighteen-year-old high on acid. The world was experiencing a paroxysm of remote pain and pleasure. Fish in the Mekong Delta feeding on Cheerios and bits of flesh; evening sunlight on a PT boat; a nearby sampan loaded with yams, and jet contrails overhead. A telephone call to Saigon from a phone booth caught in a Midwestern blizzard.

THE DEATH OF FASHION

The loss of faith in progress sparked by the Vietnam era — by military defeat, recession and the end of lunar colonization — created a traumatic vaccuum that was filled by the blossom of nostalgia. Fashion is a pure example of the process of cultural self-cannibalization that the West has embarked on. Even haute couture has to begin to feed on itself. The recent revival of Christian Dior's original designs from the fifties is part of a strong retro trend, as are some of Hubert de Givenchy's recent lines. Recycling seems to be a design principle in much of fashion these days, but there is another reason for fashion's preoccupation with the past: Western civilization itself is locked in a cycle of fast-forward nostalgia.

In the early sixties, when nostalgia for previous decades began in earnest, there was a twenties revival. By the end of the sixties, Sha Na Na, the fifties-parody group, performed at Woodstock. Sha Na Na represented a revival of music barely a decade old. This trend continued in the early seventies, with the movie *American Graffiti* and the musical *Grease* and its television spin-offs, not to mention radio stations that played "old gold." Then, in the eighties, nostalgia gained momentum with the first of the "period-mixing" films, *Blade Runner*. *Batman* and, later, *Edward Scissorhands* upped the retro ante. What was new about the period nostalgia in these films was that it encompassed the entire twentieth century; fashion from the thirties, forties, fifties, eighties and the future co-existed simultaneously. When nostalgia erupts so massively into the present, the forward movement of the historical continuum is arrested. The eighties were the decade when fashion — and, with it, "history" — ended. Period-mixing in films marked an acceleration of "retro" velocity to the point of inversion.

The Chronosphere

These days, fashions seem no longer to come and go. Instead of society as a whole undergoing a paroxysm of fashion, styles are banished to tribes. Society is being divided into enclaves of fashion devotees who live perpetually in their era. Styles such as spiked Mohawk haircuts have already been with us for over fifteen years. Even "grunge" seems to be lingering. As a result, drifting without history, we exist in a void. Because the media short-circuit the distance between desire and image, between nostalgia and retro-cachet, between irony and reverence, the speed of instant media gratification has collapsed our sense of time. McLuhan said that the electronic media had shrunk the world to a global village: however, media shrink not only space, but time, and they have shrunk cultural history to a timeless present, a media chronosphere that contains all eras.

But ours is not an effortless, wistful nostalgia. There is a restless misery in this pining for previous identities, in the search for a lost paradise of the past. Meanwhile, the skeletons are coming out of the closet. As the electronic media collapse time, they also retrieve "repressed" abuse and trauma. Not only are the old national grievances of the European mainland being resurrected — in the Balkans and elsewhere — but individuals and disadvantaged minorities are retrieving their own histories of abuse. Repressed-memory syndrome seems to operate both on a national and on an individual level, and it has become a contentious issue in the media as a result. Engulfed in these flames of nationalism and resurrected misdeeds, we exist in a timeless moment of pure, cultural consumption. Perhaps it is fitting that, at the cusp of the millennium, media culture has reached zero time.

TRANSFORMERS, MORPHING AND MUTAGENESIS

Japanese Culture and the Computer Generation

If the children born in the 1950s were the first TV generation, then the children born in the 1980s are the first computer generation. To see a child of this later generation approach any computer interface (be it IBM, Macintosh or Nintendo) is to see someone who not only is at ease with technology, but also understands its capabilities and limits. In North America, this generation is also the first that is growing up with Japanese-originated children's culture.

Peer Collectives

Japanese TV programs such as "The Mighty Morphin' Power Rangers" and "Sailor Moon" emphasize peer collectives. "Sailor Moon" (an example of the Japanese *manga* genre), for example, features one girl among a group of equals, all of whom are named after planets. In "The Mighty Morphin' Power Rangers," the submersion of the individual into a collective identity is taken one step further: when the Power Rangers "morph" into their superhero identities, their helmets make them anonymous, distinguishable only by colour. Furthermore, the customized robot vehicles they each ride in, their "Zords," can interlock and combine into a single "transformer" called a "Mega-zord."

At the risk of perpetuating the questionable deification of Japanese values, I must point out that there are some Japanese cultural differences I find compelling. For example, the Japanese emphasis on solving problems by forming collectives of equal peers is quite different from the Western tradition of individual leadership and hierarchical administrations. This difference would remain only of anthropological interest were it not for the fact that the collective method is best suited for highly technologized industries. Indeed, top-down management has turned out to be a handicap for companies building innovative technologies, whereas companies with more lateral administrations flourish. Both Apple and Microsoft had lateral hierarchies when they were first established.

But what values are being instilled into North American children by *manga* and transformers? The answer seems to be collective teamwork. The Japanese value teamwork and co-operation above everything — after all, a perfect outcome for a Japanese baseball game is a tie score. This emphasis on the collective spells the end of Western notions of "rugged individualism" and the era of the lone gunfighter. Collective culture is what has made Japan excel in the digital environment. It is a faculty that will become indispensable in the emergent networked societies of the world.

Transformers and Morphing

One aspect of Japanese children's culture that has broadly infiltrated Western consciousness is its emphasis on "transformers" and "morphing." "Transformers" are toys that unfold on hinges, changing identities in the process. "Morphing" is the transformation of a normal human into a superhero. This protean theme that originated in Japanese culture as a sort of "instant mythology" has a peculiar viability in North America. The popularity of "morphing" is not simply explained by our ancient proclivity for transformation and transcendence; its popularity also stems from a deep prescience in our children about technologies of transformation. Their fascination is more than empty techno-utopianism — these transforming scenarios are also rehearsals for the practical skills our children will need in the transhuman era. In a complex world requiring many virtual selves, a single, inflexible identity may well turn out to be a handicap.

Transformers represent a new alternative for humanity

insofar as they embody the potential to change shape according to necessity. This is a shift from our standard primate approach of being physical generalists, able to adapt to many tasks. Children, whose minds are flexible enough to grasp the essence of complex technological changes, are foresightful in this way — their toys are harbingers of a new relationship to our bodies that will be much more receptive to physical augmentation and transformation. Perhaps the recent proliferation of plastic surgery of all types is the first indication of this new view of the body.

Obscured by the managerial truisms that have recently been pronounced about Japanese industrial capability, the Japanese cultural influence is almost invisible — possibly because, with the exception of karaoke, it has been exported primarily to children. The Japanese, with their exquisitely adaptive culture, have intuited the direction of human technological evolution and its effect on identity. This identity change will include not only a greater sense of collective enterprise, but also the proliferation of multiple personalities, for multiple identities will be a standard feature of the transhuman era.

PSYCHEDELIC MUTAGENESIS

Japanese culture has not been alone in its anticipation of the technology-induced trend towards "morphing" and transformation. The West experienced its first brush with mutagenesis (mutating into new forms) during the psychedelic era, from 1965 to 1975. At that time, many individuals who had taken LSD claimed that they had transformed into a new species. (Later this notion was taken to its literalized limit in

Ken Russell's film *Altered States*.) The myth of the psyche-delic era was that the new consciousness vouchsafed us by LSD would turn users into "new creatures" who would change the world.

In early psychedelic literature, such as Thomas De Quincy's *Confessions of an English Opium-Eater* (1822), the metaphor for the psychedelic experience was one of travel: the hashish user "visited" exotic realms. Only during the 1960s, with the writings of Timothy Leary and the resurgence of interest in Aldous Huxley, did the notion of personal transformation and alteration of consciousness become linked with the psyche-delic experience. The romanticizing of "mutants" dates back to that period. Hippies happily referred to themselves as "freaks." The psychedelic era laid the necessary groundwork for the second wave of interest in mutagenesis that is being catalysed by the digital revolution.

LSD and the Continuing Psychedelic Revolution

The effects of the psychedelic revolution are still reverberat-ing through our culture. The layers of reality glimpsed by those who experienced altered states have permeated society. One small step for Aldous Huxley and Timothy Leary was one giant step for popular culture. Though only a few entered the psychedelic realm, the rest of us went with them because of our connection to the "datasphere," our collective media world. Everything, from the animation sequences on "Sesame Street" to rock videos, bears the unmistakable stamp of psychedelia.

The Glass Onion

It may be that our cultural proclivity for past eras is another inheritance from the psychedelic era. The way we perceive time and history was one of the first casualties of the psychedelic revolution. The Beatles, for example, who mediated their LSD experiences with their music, underwent an intense retrospective period, a kind of auto-nostalgia, that popular culture amplified. During the late sixties, previous eras became metaphors for the layering of our own psyches, the glass-onion effect. Western culture underwent a collective reconsideration of the formation of its identity. Perhaps this contributed to the acceleration of retro-nostalgia in the early seventies.

Multiple Personalities

Psychedelic drugs also allowed a recombination of identity in a way that foreshadowed the mutations that cyberspace is starting to impose on us. Being in several places at once is easier if each location can be tagged with a different identity. Today, single careers seem to be a thing of the past. Tomorrow, multiple personalities, several identities within one person, might become both recreational and professional necessities. Different identities also allow the flexibility necessary for perpetual transformation, as, increasingly, rigid identities will become an impediment to the acquisition of skills, experiences and power.

TERATOLOGY

Teratology, the study of monsters and freaks of nature, aptly describes our pre-millennial penchant for fantastic creatures. We have become a culture of teratophiles, fascinated by grotesques and by mutants, aliens and deviants. Because we are on the verge of self-directed physical mutation, the inventory of chimeras we are building is a library of potential forms. We are broadening the palette of the possible in terms of human appearance.

Freaks are of compelling interest for our media culture because they are possibly the forms that await us. Already we are employing them as cybermorphs and avatars, the shapes we use to represent ourselves in cyberspace. Eventually they might even become the embodied repositories for posthumans. Our current fascination with the extremes of human form has habituated us to the "alien." At the same time, paradoxically, we are becoming more sensitized to individual human variation and to racial distinctions, though not in a hierarchical, racist sense. As we begin to control human variation with biotechnology, our forms will become more and more exaggerated, as they reflect the freedom of virtual bodily transformation in cyberspace. This teratogenesis is being accelerated by computers and catalysed by their mutative force.

THE MEME GENERATION

The most prolific source of cultural transformation over the past thirty years has been the "meme" generation. In Richard Dawkins's book, *The Selfish Gene*, he gives the name "memes" (rhymes with "themes") to concepts or ideas that are imitated and taken up collectively by groups of humans, like cultural genes. Memes are consensually viable ideas, concepts and inventions that are perpetuated by societies, not just by individuals. They are, in a sense, our mental inheritance. Dawkins defines memes as individual units of behaviour that reproduce themselves via human minds. Examples of memes are catch phrases, CD-players, fashions, religious beliefs, and tools.

The age group that breeds the most popular-cultural memes comprises those between eighteen and twenty-eight. Always. Members of this group have just mastered our culture from the inside out, and they have the advantage of having grown up within the media landscape of the day rather than having watched it develop as outsiders, as older generations must. They also have the remnant security of being recent members of a family unit, and this gives them their special revolutionary momentum as they become part of the larger society.

Western culture has not, however, become "youth-focused," a fact that was statistically obscured by the questionable demographics of the baby boom; what happened instead is that the media began, in the mid-1950s, to give more coverage to the culture of late adolescence and early adulthood. As a result, the meme generation was able for the first time to take their rightful place in the cultural spotlight. Rock 'n' roll was the signal of their coming of age.

Being Ahead of Your Time

The influence of the meme generation on fashion and, consequently, on the clothing industry, is increasingly being recognized. Major clothing and shoe companies hire agents called "coolhunters" to keep track of what trend-setting kids wear in big cities in order to determine which styles will become popular. Meme spawning, which is intrinsic to cultural industry, is a fickle and unpredictable process, however. You have to be *just* ahead of your time, just a *little* more intelligent, to be successful. Too far ahead, and you leave everyone behind, including your audience. No one likes that. If you are too prescient, you might achieve the same fate as the genius avant-garde — time machines burning out in their own private future.

BODY PIERCING AS INVOCATION OF THE CYBORG

It could very well be that the recent fascination with body piercing is a celebratory premonition of the eventual fusion of human flesh with machines. Perhaps body piercing, with its roots in the punk-rock movement of the late seventies, is a cosmetic invocation of the cyborg. Certainly our species is proceeding with medical prostheses of all sorts: artificial joints, pacemakers, and so on. Increasingly we are incorporating synthetic parts as replacements and extensions of our bodies, and this process will continue and expand incrementally.

On an individual level, body piercing is not an imposition or invasion as much as it is an intervention, a constant reminder of the delicious state of being "of flesh," of being incarnate — perpetually wounded, impaled by silver and gold, by materiality. Like tattooing, body piercing is a generational signal, the pierced eyebrow signifying membership in a select caste of young adults; but, unlike tattooing, it is highly personal and intimate. Tattoos are digital identifications, like bar codes for the initiated; they are not tribal markings or decorations, though they have that concept deep within their genealogy. Body piercing signifies the paradox of a generation unwilling to be placed in categories, yet, at the same time, eager to embrace mass trends.

TRANSITIONAL TECHNOLOGY SKILLS

During periods of rapid technological change, many transitional technologies and operating procedures are developed, and then made obsolescent. We are entering a period of disposable skills, a vast meme landfill of the concepts and routines that we learned for use with various obsolete devices. It is the sheer scale of this dispensability — all the repertoires and behaviour that we jettison yearly — that is impressive. Early Internet protocols from the late eighties would be incomprehensible to anyone getting on the Net now. Similarly, we no longer need to learn Commodore 64 keycodes in the age of Windows. And whatever happened to the world champion of Pac Man?

Paradoxically, ignorance and unfamiliarity will give certain individuals the edge over people who *will have to unlearn* their old procedures *as well as learn* new ones. Ignorance will be speed. Interdisciplinarily educated electronic engineers, *without* prior exposure to contemporary electronic products, will become a valuable resource for digital companies, like hunting falcons kept blind until their hoods are removed.

PSYCHIC MATERIALISM

Media-based advertising comprises an electronic, global catalogue in which all the world's merchandise is displayed. When everything is up for sale, then only those things that cannot be purchased have any value: personal experiences, having a muscular or lean body, specialized knowledge, famous friends — these are some of the things that are beyond purchase. The previous sanctuaries of privilege and wealth — possessions, lifestyles, designer labels and European cars — are gone because they are no longer exotic. All the icons of wealth have been aped by popular culture: the suburbs are now full of BMWs, nannies and Giorgio Armani suits.

High culture and taste still retain their cachet, but high culture is increasingly commodified, and taste is still a dangerous territory, fraught with uncertainty. (After all, a client without taste has no way of determining whether or not the consultants she hires have taste themselves.) As the once exclusive icons of wealth and privilege become commonplace, the confession of moral indiscretions and past misdeeds becomes not only redemptive, but fashionable. Celebrities confess their indiscretions almost as soon as they commit them, and, even more appalling still, childhood traumas become exotic possessions — not only are they beyond duplication by other adult celebrities vying for attention, but they also portray the confessor as a victim, which is possibly the highest value that our culturally exhausted society can confer within the voyeuristic impulses of its psychic materialism. This travesty of victimhood is doubly pernicious because it obscures society's ability to discern real victims at a time when innocence is at a premium.

THE END OF PRIVACY IN THE DIGITAL AGE

The electronic media have blended the division between the public and private realms, and as a result the private lives of media
personalities have become the subject of intense scrutiny. Because
celebrities' images are formed by the mass media, the public consider it paradoxical that the famous should have any private lives
whatsoever. Furthermore, because television is so hungry for
"documentary data" (which Madonna was clever to exploit in her
pseudo-documentary *Truth Or Dare*), the private lives of stars
and politicians are even more fascinating than they were before
the advent of television. Princess Diana, in consequence, became
a tragic casualty of the weight of the world's attention upon her:
in a kind of media Heisenberg effect the world destroyed what it
was looking at by the very act of looking. So much for the privacy
of public lives, but what of personal privacy?

Individual privacy might come to an end as soon as digital
society no longer requires it. Present-day notions of personal
freedom and privacy, extolled by a range of social thinkers,
from Rousseau to Chomsky, might become obsolete. But privacy will not end because a nightmare consortium of corporations and "big brother" bureaucracies will use new
technology to investigate individual consumer-citizens
(although new technology will certainly be complicit in the
disappearance of privacy); rather, privacy will end only when
emergent forms of digital consciousness transcend the entire
set of rules that have hitherto governed the interactions (and
the definitions) of individuals and groups. In other words,
information that we now consider private — such as our
income or what we do when we are alone — we may come to
consider as public within transhuman collectives.

The end of personal privacy will also mark our transcendence of a moral system based on proprietary and territorial notions of privacy. At present, violations of our confidential identity are viewed as aggressions; we see them as contrary to the sanctity of the individual. The "self" is a private domain to be defended at all costs. It is, in the end, a type of colonial enclave or freehold to which we feel we have sovereign rights. For this reason, privacy is linked with notions of individual freedom, and so it follows that other people's knowledge of you or your activities diminishes your potential freedom, particularly if these people decide to restrict it. That is why militant libertarianism and encryption (cypher punks) have become central themes of the digital age.

But the tide of technological linkage is flowing in the opposite direction, and notions of privacy will, consequently, be radically redefined. As humans continue to interconnect, and the power of electronic collectives begins to be felt, we will probably abandon territorial notions of self in the rush to contribute to the transformation of human consciousness. It may well be that the experience of collective consciousness, nascent in our telecommunications cocoon, will be so exhilarating that our eventual participation in meta-conscious entities (whose consciousness might be to ours as ours is to animals') will be wholly voluntary.

Chapter 2

PROPERTIES OF MEDIA

PRINCIPLES OF MEDIA

Anything that carries a signal any distance is a medium. Sunlight is an elemental medium. Photons deliver shadow information about the objects between the Earth and the Sun — be they dust particles, asteroids or the Moon. We carry neurological media in our bodies. Our nervous systems are intimate media relaying signals from our fingertips to our brains, and vice versa. Most human artifacts are also media, transmitting cultural signals. Clothes are media of sorts, as are houses.

FOUNDATION MEDIA

Any kind of reconstituted environment is a form of medium. Clothes are screens for our projected fashion fantasies. Even the first huts, made of sticks and leaves, were synthetic environments. The components of their interiors — structural ribs forming identical and repeated elements, and an artificially enclosed space — comprised a proto-architecture. Along with tools and containers, huts marked a reordering of the natural environment. This new environment made meta-environments, environments within environments, possible. Plumbing systems are another kind of humble medium. Every citizen connected to a water main lives on the banks of a mechanical river whose waters are ingeniously forced into pipes and valves.

Contemporary buildings are structural media as well as mechanisms. Artificial environments constituted by both the interiors and the exteriors of buildings are powerful media. The geometry and decorative abstractions of architecture are visual environments that form a sort of static medium. The individual buildings themselves are a constituent part of the artificial, geometric landscape of cities.

MEDIA PSYCHOLOGY

According to McLuhan, communications technologies and electronic media not only extend our nervous systems, but also have corollary, reciprocal effects on the nervous systems they extend. While new media are amplifying or extending our capabilities, they are simultaneously modifying us as we adapt to them.

We accommodate media on two levels: physical and mental. The physical accommodations, such as having to hold a telephone to the ear, or place our hands on a keyboard to operate a computer, are obvious. The psychological accommodations are more subtle and nebulous. Media affect our nervous systems and, in turn, our psychology. Media such as television excite our nervous systems and make us manic. Radios are comforting and, at low volume, lulling. Portable

CD-players are excitatory. Each medium has a mood, or field of influence on our nervous systems, and every technology has a psychological effect to be considered along with its social and physical effects.

RAW ELECTRIC CURRENT

At the source of all electronic media is the deep, nervous tactility of raw current: unedited electricity itself — crackling, painful, dangerous and quick. The sudden purple-white branches of lightning in electrical storms. Subway trains sparking blue. The scent of smoke and ozone. Lightning in the wires. The exquisite, metallic sourness of pure DC current tingling the end of your tongue when you touch it to the tip of a nine-volt battery. The quick, shivering eels of current slipping into any conductor they can find, darting through water and nerves. Electric shock. The red glow of heating elements excited to incandescence by electron friction. The live wire, the shorted light-switch, and the rippling muscle spasms of pure current travelling up the arm. A pinprick of static electricity on a dry, winter day.

The Generic Signal

Whether it travels from satellite-dish to monitor or from amplifier to speaker, an electronic signal is generic. It is essential only that the signal be transmitted. It is all or nothing. In practice, electronic equipment is also generic — a forty-five-inch TV and a four-inch portable both receive and reproduce identical signals; an expensive computer cruises the same Net a cheap one does. This indicates that an innate egalitarianism is hard-wired into electronic media.

Unlike purely mechanical devices, the paths of electrons through circuits are only somewhat affected by product quality. If the functional specifications are identical, then brand name is unimportant. Software is equally impartial, and a cloned software system is like a generic drug — its programmer is irrelevant as far as its users are concerned. The formula, not the source of the formula, is the product.

LUMINESCENT MEDIA

Incandescent Light

The light from an incandescent bulb is also a form of medium. Its content is both ambience (the light in our rooms) and data — with flickers and occasional variations in brightness, the incandescent bulb conveys information about other users and the power grid that supplies it. These subtle modulations of the incandescent bulb's intensity alert us that it is part of an electrical network, whether the source of that network is a nearby generator or a hydro-electric power grid.

Although incandescent light is softer and yellower than fluorescent light, it does not reproduce the light thrown by a candle. A candle's flame is form and process at the same time, and thus complete in itself. A light bulb is only a conversion unit, a photon-dispersion device, the projector of a distant electrical signal.

The presence of an incandescent light bulb is predicated on both a viewer and a scene to be illuminated. The light bulb signals that there is a content within its light, something to look at. It is, after all, light to see by. The circle of illumination is a phenomenological theatre, even if it is deserted or there is no one there to see it. (This quality is often exploited as a stage device in theatre. A single lamp illuminating part of a stage invariably sets up audience expectations of impending drama.) Anything within the perimeter of incandescent light is a narrative, particularly at night, and especially outdoors. Any natural setting illuminated by a light bulb (and this quality is shared by spotlights and halogen bulbs) becomes a spectacle. Night-time baseball and tennis games have a slightly surreal aspect for this reason.

Fluorescent Light

Fluorescent light, particularly the cool white fluorescent light in offices, is the great bleakness. Radiating primarily on the yellow and violet wavelengths of visible light, fluorescence is a caricature of light, enough only to read and work by. A candle, seen through the "eye" of a full-spectrum camera, appears brighter beside most fluorescent lights because it radiates in all the major colours of the spectrum: green, blue, and red as well as yellow and violet.

Fluorescent light is anorexic light. Food retailers discovered in the seventies that food in coolers under fluorescent lights spoiled faster than that beneath incandescent lights.

Fluorescent light pulsates differently from incandescent light, primarily because of the excited gas within the tubes. Fluorescent lighting is display lighting par excellence for the interiors of large department stores and office buildings, being both cheap and explicit. It is an erotic light. Living creatures, including humans, look exotic in the desert of fluorescent light. By rendering everything within its illumination into a product on display, fluorescent light objectifies the human body. Perhaps this is why offices, libraries and government buildings sometimes create such intense sexual-fantasy lives in their employees.

Fluorescent lighting is particularly effective when it is used at night in window display cases, where its bleak, commodified radiance is confined to a lucent cube of glass.

Halogen and Neon Light

Halogen light is produced by a tungsten filament in halogen gas. Halogens cast hard-edge shadows, which heighten the theatricality of their light but also make it more solitary. Halogen light has a wider spectrum than the light produced by fluorescent tubes and vapour lamps. The intense, piercing halogen headlights of luxury cars, with their diamond brilliance, signal power — the radiance of imperious scrutiny.

Neon light is excited atomic gas radiating pure electric colours. Neon light is visible electric current. It pulses and is highly sensual, particularly in a combination of blue and red. Neon is the fire within; it is its own content, separate from what it illuminates. Neon is the tactile experience of colour and light as pure sensation.

THERMODYNAMIC MEDIA

Refrigerators, air conditioners and heating systems are thermodynamic media, and heat is the signal that is transferred.

Refrigerators

A refrigerator is an illuminated gallery, a grocery display in an alpine microclimate. A refrigerator is also a meditative shrine, a domestic contemplative icon. Before an opened refrigerator, we stand mesmerized, our hand on the door, staring into the myriad possibilities and combinations of foodstuffs. We are hypnotized by the tableau of package designs and colours, the cool theatre of imminent satisfaction.

A freezer is a time capsule. Last year's green beans, flash-boiled and frozen, taste almost as good as they did when picked. Freezers are chronological wine cellars of nostalgia, whether they contain the frozen chicken picked up two months ago at the farmers' market or the six-month-old chocolate ice cream growing a beard of ice crystals. The freezer holds an embryo of the ice age.

Air Conditioners

Air conditioners turn rooms and houses into microclimates. The way the air has been cooled, however, conditions the ambience in more ways than just the lowering of temperature. Air-conditioned coldness feels like it comes from the industrial cave darkness of a northern mountain. There is a special quality to air-conditioned rooms, a spidery, tingly coolness that some people find intolerable, even on the hottest days. Air conditioners are also white-noise generators; their sound breeds a torrent of auditory hallucinations. Apparently the brain manufactures meaning out of certain kinds of noise. Many people report hearing faint voices and music when they are on the verge of sleep in an air-conditioned room.

Wind In the Walls: Ventilation and Heating Systems

Air conditioners are just one of several microclimatological media. Any kind of processed air, issuing from a ventilator shaft, say, or a forced-air vent, constitutes an atmospheric medium, replete with almost all the subliminal effects that electronic media have. Forced-air and building ventilation systems deliver piped wind. Their content is their temperature, the pressure variables of the fan, and exotic air from various levels of a building.

MICROWAVE OVENS

Because they use extreme radio signals to cook food, microwave ovens are infra-broadcasting radio stations. Just as digital access in our CD-players introduced us to instant musical gratification, our food can now be cooked as if it were digital, the LCD display counting out digital roasting units.

PUBLIC-ADDRESS SYSTEMS: AURALTECTURAL SPACE

By enclosing the audience in the amplified personal intimacy of the microphone, public-address systems become live broadcasts; they are acoustic shells that embrace listeners in an aural, tactile space. Because these shells are so coddling, they retrieve childhood freedom and invulnerability — hence, "mosh pits," violent-contact zones at rock concerts, where the participants feel that no physical harm can befall them. Conversely, the PA system simulates parental authority (as politicians discovered early in the twentieth century), and this, as much as their convenience, ensures that they regulate and command schools, businesses and airports.

CD-PLAYERS

Instead of reproducing music, digitized compact discs represent music. (The sound of a live symphony orchestra is analog, not digital.) Digital sound does not occur naturally in the real world. It is, rather, a series of recorded samples that are turned into quantized values. The sampling occurs at a rate faster than the human ear can detect; even though the music is only a series of bits, there is more information in the digitized version than we actually require. An audio critic once said that listening to digitized music was like going to a restaurant and eating the menu, except that, in this case, the menu tastes better than the food.

The real impact CD-players have had, however, is on the way we listen to music. With tape decks and, to a lesser extent, record players, music was sequential and linear, almost like ROM (read-only-memory in computers), and songs could be accessed only in a fixed order. CD-players gave us RAM (random-access-memory) music, allowing us instant access to any song. On a compact disc, any sequence of music exists simultaneously with other sequences. The music search becomes a tree search, like hypertext or linked Web pages.

Digital systems favour digital music, and digital music is purest when it uses synthesized sounds. With their purely electronic tones, synthesizers seem ideal for digital reproduction.

As well, synthesized music has a vaguely hallucinatory effect on CD listeners because it is composed of truly artificial sounds never heard in nature. Synthesized music is music made mathematical, sound halfway to ideal thought and space. Perhaps that is why the frictionless, zero-gravity of synthesized music — presented digitally on its own dedicated carrier — is mesmerizing. The "trance" music played at "raves" oscillates to this specific, digital frequency.

TELEPHONES

Communications media distort the user's perception of time. For example, callers tend to underestimate the amount of time they spend on the telephone. It takes twice as much time to be in two places at once, and, in the economy of telecommunications, media telepresence is what takes up the "missing time." But the telephone is not only a mediator of foreshortened time, it is also one of the most sensual of telecommunications devices because the ear is such an intimate orifice. The telephone conjures an erotic potential by placing a discarnate mouth against the ear. The recent proliferation of phone sex is a testament to its implicit sensuality.

TELEVISION

Television is a fluid. It is as if TV screens are full of television "liquid," so that dark rooms lit solely by television sets look like they are underwater. Because television is a fluid, we bathe in it, we "channel surf."

Like a family friend abandoned in another room, television is a low-grade party that can be left on its own. It is hypnotic. Colour television gentrifies interiors. Instead of renovating a run-down cocktail bar, many proprietors install more colour TVs. The interior surfaces of the bar, reflecting the hallucinatory waves of TV colour, are washed in a patina of electric glamour.

Broadcast Television and Films

Because broadcast television is continuous, you can only sample television; even when you turn off your set, broadcast television is still going. Broadcast television is like a river, a current; it has more in common with electric light than with film. Films, which have a beginning and an end, are more like books. It is not coincidental that flip-books and films achieve the same effect. This is not to say you cannot have a "cinematic experience" with television. True, movies on video can be almost as satisfying as movies at the theatre, but the video experience is intrinsically different from that of watching film.

Chapter 3

TELEVISION

HOW ELECTRON-SCAN TELEVISION MIMICS CONSCIOUSNESS

Television, with its constant scene shifts, requires continuous (usually subconscious) orienting responses from the viewer. There are on average twelve jump-cuts a minute during a regular network drama, twenty jump-cuts a minute during commercials, and upwards of sixty jump-cuts a minute during some rock videos and movie trailers. If you pay attention, you can count these shifts, because they take place well within human response time. However, the scan of the electron beam which builds the whole television image two-and-a-half times a second is on another time scale altogether. The flicker of the electron-scanning beam stimulates the flicker of electrical activity in the conscious brain. As mesmerizing as these two flash rates are (the jump-cuts and the electron-scanning cycle), the electron scan has an additional effect that makes television so very compelling.

Our consciousness is highly selective. We look only at a small sample of the complete visual reality, and our subconscious mind fills in the rest. During any given half-second, well below the threshold of conscious perception — but not below the threshold of unconscious perception — a TV image is incomplete. The electron-scanning beam lays down the lines of the television image like a fast bricklayer and an entire screen is "built up" a little more than twice a second. Although the interval between the incomplete screens is sub-liminal, TV is always missing something, something that we unconsciously feel compelled to fill in. (You can observe the action of the electron scan by tilting your head forty-five degrees and moving your eyes quickly from left to right, to points above and below the television screen. The screen image should contract to a white line.) The continuity of tele-vision that we consciously perceive is an optical illusion. In reality, what the nervous system and brain see, before the conscious mind consolidates it, is only a ghostly flicker.

THE PSYCHOLOGY OF MANIPULATION

Afternoon Talk Shows and TV Advertising

Broadcast television is not individually interactive, but it is col-lectively interactive, for if television is a "public mind" (as Bill Moyers called it), it is also a window onto mass psychology, particularly as we work out our collective moral and psycho-logical transformations. Broadcast television is a public forum where we air our fantasies and concerns. Afternoon talk shows, in particular, with their carefully selected studio audiences and host/therapist, comprise a highly manipulated psychological exegesis of collective concerns. In a sense, afternoon talk shows are like explicit, interactive commercials in that they use the strategies of television marketing — moral ambiguity, opinion polls, manipulated surveys and subtle psychological biases.

There is a peculiar symbiosis at work here, because at the same time as our nascent collective consciousness is dealing, via afternoon talk shows, with notions of public morality and personal freedoms (such as cross-dressing and multiple relationships), advertisers are using the most sophisticated tools of modern psychology available to them to manipulate us with the same issues. The cumulative effect of advertising's overt psychological assault on the audience is to unconsciously reinforce the psychological pathologies that advertising "plays" on, the same concerns that provide the content for afternoon talk shows. Advertisers in television and magazines in recent times have resorted to even more pathological "hooks," relying on the visual suggestion of a range of quasi-neurotic (but common) aberrant behaviours — from obsession to stalking, from voyeurism to pedophilia, as the notorious Calvin Klein ads of 1996 amply illustrated.

FOLK SURVEILLANCE: THE CAMCORDER INSURGENCY

Audience manipulation by broadcast television is being partly redressed by home video. The proliferation of camcorders is a demographic revolution that is just starting to make itself felt. A decade or two ago, access to television cameras was limited to stations with sufficient resources to purchase recording and broadcasting equipment. Now, camcorders, in the hands of ordinary citizens, have expanded the scope of television and television journalism. The ubiquity of handycams has led to a kind of folk surveillance that acts as a partial antidote to the consensual illusions of media journalism. Citizen videos comprise a powerful, decentralized network, and it is implicitly political. We are now beginning to film all the dark corners of our society, and what we see is frightening us. The ever-increasing amount of handycam footage that is finding its way onto prime-time news is prompting a social/political power shift. Big Brother is here, and he is us.

Every new technology creates contradictory social possibilities for either oppression or emancipation. Camcorders can enhance personal freedom and civil rights by documenting abuses of power, and thereby become a force of emancipation, or they can be a tool for institutional oppression — governments and corporations using video surveillance of citizens and workers. Several small towns in both England and the United States have chosen to augment their under-staffed police departments with complete video-surveillance systems whose monitors are viewed by citizen volunteers.

Nevertheless, ubiquitous camcorders seem to support a bottom-up democracy wherein individual citizens can police their governments but the government cannot use public surveillance, as effectively, to police their citizens. Recently, in western Canada, a police department compiled video-surveillance clips from a youth riot involving looting and property damage that had occurred after a sporting event. The clips were exhibited at interactive-video kiosks in several malls, and citizens were encouraged to enter the names of anyone they recognized on the surveillance video. What the police didn't take into account was the nature of a voyeuristic medium like television: culpability has only one direction with interactive television — bottom up, not top down. Very few individuals co-operated.

Sensitization, Nationalism and the Military

At the same time as camcorders are helping us to examine ourselves more explicitly than ever before, we, at least, we North Americans, are becoming more and more sensitized to violence. This phenomenon involves another property of media — namely, that the media engender in their audience paradoxical tendencies, creating the inverse of the expected effect. For example, electronic globalization has led to nationalism instead of world harmony. In the same way, constant exposure to graphic film violence should brutalize us, but, paradoxically, we are becoming newly sensitized to real violence. We are shocked by camcorder footage of police beatings, military hazing rituals and street violence, as if this were all new to us.

North America could become the biggest electronic-surveillance state since cold-war Russia, but it seems more likely that the inherent libertarianism of the electronic media will ensure we maintain a truly egalitarian and democratic society. One hopes that this public surveillance will lead to greater accountability of government to the populace. Instances of corruption, abuse of power and state brutality will simply not be allowed to continue under such scrutiny. Imagine what might happen if the public at large decided that governmentally sponsored genocide, that is, armies killing foreign citizens, was morally intolerable. When mass audiences *emotionally* understand the total depravity of killing another human being, even if that murder is governmentally sanctioned, there will be consequences, among them a repugnance similar to that instilled by news footage of the Vietnam War, but qualitatively different because of the new credibility and paradoxical sensitization of audiences at the turn of the millennium. I would like to imagine that it won't be long before citizens question the whole premise of armed conflict.

TELEVISION IN THE FLAT-SCREEN ERA

Although the introduction of high-definition digital TV (HDTV) will alter how we respond to television, its effect will be minimal compared with the overall impact that flat-screen technology will have. The advent of large flat screens, whether they use back-lit liquid-crystal-display or plasma-screen technology, will revolutionize the way we watch television, and possibly the very content of TV programming. Although we can expect considerable changes in our response to television with the arrival of convergence (the much-touted unification of television, telephones, computers and the Internet), those wrought by the flat screen will be more fundamental. Television's mechanics of mesmerization — the hypnotic dance of the scanning electron beam — will disappear, and, with it, the whole context and rationale for much of today's television content. Even if the images on large, flat screens look identical to those on scanning-electron TVs in terms of brightness and sharpness, our nervous systems do not respond to them in the same way at all. This is part of the reason for consumer and industry resistance to flat screens. Flat-screen television will not be television, at least as we currently know it.

First of all, flat screens are "quiet;" they do not have any of the frenzied flicker of electron-scanning screens and will be less engaging because they do not clamour for perceptual attention in the same way. The static flat screen, which eliminates subconscious interactivity, will "distance" viewers in a profound way. Television, and television advertising, will become much less compelling, and viewers will be much more ambivalent. Consumer choice will thereby be enhanced, and both advertisers and programmers will have to change their pitch radically to compensate for the effects of flat screens.

Flat screens will affect literacy as well. The flat screen is much more like a page than a screen, and its "quietness" will be more hospitable to literary media. This influence may well counter the effects of computer voice-recognition and work to maintain current literacy levels.

Chapter 4

ADVERTISING:
The Politics of Perception

METAPHORS IN THE MEDIA

During the recession of the early 1990s, a series of public metaphors was used to describe the progress of the economy. The forum in which these metaphors were most prolific was the television news broadcast. At the beginning of the recession, anchors stated that "the economy is fragile." In this metaphor, our economy was characterized as a substance that had become brittle and weak. As the recession deepened, a sense of alarm began to appear, revealed in such statements as "It's a scraping-along-the-bottom scenario" — the economy had become a submerged vehicle sliding on the ocean floor — and "We've hit the skids" — the economy was again a vehicle, but now careening towards disaster.

Then real despair began to emerge, with such images as "The economy is flat on its back" that depicted the economy as a boxer who had been knocked out, or "The economy continues to flounder," where a marine analogy is again invoked. This latter type of metaphor was a popular one; it also yielded "Our government will stay on course with present fiscal policy." Sometimes the economy was compared to an internal-combustion engine: "The engine of the economy is still stalled" or "We need something to kick-start the economy."

When signs of "recovery" (as if the economy was a sick patient) emerged, we became travellers "on the road to recovery," a metaphor wherein the economy resembled an ambulatory out-patient rather than a bed-ridden in-patient. At this time the economy was also likened to an object that had been facing in the wrong direction: "The economy is beginning to turn around."

When the economy began to "flounder" again, new metaphors were called in. The economy was now an object that had been struck by another, as in "There has been some impact of the global economy on the current situation." Television news anchors, resurrecting the engine analogy, declared "The economy continues to sputter" or "We've hit a speed-bump on the road to recovery." Once again, the economy became the weary traveller — "The economy continues to stumble" — and, finally, as we began to "climb out of the recession" (recession as pit), the economy became a patient again: "The strength of the recovery is feeble."

As the Berkeley linguist George Lakoff has said, our consensual metaphors define us, and, more than that, they define how we will deal with our problems as a society; we can be effective in dealing with our collective problems only if we characterize them effectively. Consensual metaphors are much more than a barometer of mass psychology; they condition society into adopting viewpoints that determine how it will respond to various crises. The metaphors that the media used during the recession seemed to connote a listless, victimized resignation to economic forces. Perhaps the fact that the recession was as protracted as it was is attributable to that very characterization.

ASSOCIATIVE CONDITIONING IN TELEVISION ADVERTISING

Television commercials employ several modes of representation, depending on the product being advertised. These modes are determined by the nature of consumer desire for that commodity, how quickly and cheaply that desire can be satisfied (by purchase or consumption), and whether the pleasure derived from consumption is physical (therefore, not gender-specific) or sexual/hormonal (therefore, gender-specific).

For example, consumable products that satisfy short-term bodily cravings such as hunger are often displayed temptingly, unadorned and without the mediation of an overlay of the usual associative devices, for example, the overlay of sex in car commercials. Food is photographed lusciously and in large quantities, usually in a social setting, with people happily enjoying it. Very occasionally food is advertised by hyperbole, and sometimes by reference to its origin. Bowls of fruit represent fruit juice, wheat sheaves and raw grain suggest breakfast cereals, and giant chunks of chocolate represent the chocolate chips in cookies. Candy, however, unlike breakfast cereal or restaurants, is often marketed by associative techniques that compare it to recreational drugs.

Associative techniques are used almost exclusively for certain items. Cars, alcoholic beverages and package holidays are sold by associative fantasies. This type of association is metaphoric and oblique: nothing is what it seems. In candy commercials, addictive behaviour is suggested by having couples fight over chocolate bars. Addictive desperation was also suggested by the chocolate bar commercials of the early nineties that used the candy as bait on hooks controlled by fish. Caffeinated soft drinks and chewing-gum also fall into the same recreational-drug category. Witness the ecstatic cola drinkers and the speedy, bouncy gum-chewers.

Some genres of television advertising seem, at first glance, not to use associative techniques at all. Practical items — such as floor-care products, toothpastes, skin creams and car wax — are often promoted by means of "scientific" demonstrations and comparisons, but such approaches are really another type of associative technique, one that enlists scientific credibility. By purchasing the advertised product, you are benefiting from scientific progress, and you can take satisfaction from your own enlightened choice.

The hard core of pseudo-science, however, is reserved for non-prescription pharmaceuticals. The diagrams of the digestive tract that promote stomach preparations, the charts showing the effectiveness of pain relievers, and the before-and-after comparisons of cold sufferers turn us, the consumers, into weekend diagnosticians administering sophisticated medicines. It is here, among these purportedly benign products, that we encounter one of the more sinister border-blurs in associative advertising — namely, where pseudo-medicine acts as a cover for the marketing of soporific concoctions or "cold remedies" that make up the

bulk of over-the-counter-drug sales. Some of these drugs promote borderline substance abuse. Disguised as remedies, they
are associatively marketed on television as recreational drugs,
a tall order for a thirty-second spot.

Associative television advertising is a particular favourite
with marketers of cars; alcohol; snacks and soft drinks; and
beauty, personal-hygiene and household-cleaning products.
You don't simply buy a car, you acquire a more affluent
lifestyle — you can afford to take leisurely, solo drives by the
ocean during midweek afternoons when no other cars are on
the road. Similarly, you're not purchasing a hair conditioner,
you're the director of a successful dance company with a
good-looking, easily controlled boyfriend. You're not buying
a beer, you're making lots of kooky friends to accompany you
to great parties. This isn't wine, it is a hot relationship with a
sexy blond. You're not purchasing a household cleanser,
you're joining a worldwide ecological movement. You may
think you're picking up men's deodorant from your local
cosmetic counter, but actually you are ensuring male bonding with athletic executives who play racquetball. That mini-
van is really family togetherness. Caffeinated cola is a
multiracial sex party. Chewing-gum can enhance your
income; it is usually enjoyed on yachts and in expensive
houses. Pick-up trucks are male-hormone boosters. Hair dye
is self-confidence. Laundry detergent promotes harmony
and bonding in the nuclear family.

By harnessing behavioural psychology, advertising has triv-
ialized our aspirations, as well as our standards of personal
achievement, in relation to family, identity and sexuality.

THE DOORS OF DECEPTION

The visual hyperbole that pervades our culture has conditioned us to accept travesties of perception. Images are doctored to look "more natural" than they actually are: teeth are whiter, sunsets are redder. As a result, citizens of Western techno-industrial states no longer perceive reality. Like stage productions, mass-entertainment media and advertising have developed a shorthand vocabulary of larger-than-life symbols. They have created a synthetic inventory of artificial images — a hypo-realism that is turning the world into a cartoon caricature of itself.

The media are constantly trying to give us the "look and feel" of something. To do this, they take "ambience" samples, or news samples, or selectively sample a personality they are trying to "profile" in order to present something that appears genuine (in television, trying to "correct" for the medium's unreality requires overcompensation) or that feels genuine within the media sketch of reality. Their personal illusion is the "inside story." Unfortunately, given a consensual autocracy, the inside story is merely an illusory scrim designed to bolster the values and beliefs we already hold.

Advertising and Surrealism

Advertising is supernatural, that is, more than natural, and the product being promoted is elevated, singled out, given a significance that exceeds or is outside the natural order. That is why surrealism is advertising's most natural mode. Tricks of the eye, *trompe l'oeil*, make what everyone knows — that advertising creates its own reality — explicit. What would seem bizarre or surreal in ordinary reality is commonplace in the advertising realm: cars that fly, crowns materializing on the heads of diners, all sorts of magical transformations and surrealities. Advertising is naturally surreal because its associations are dream-like.

DIGITAL PACKAGING

Digital networks will be a packaging dream. There will be nothing to ship and there will be no delivery logistics: no trucks, inventories, warehouses, only virtual packages. Digital products will be ideal advertising commodities because the product, the package and the advertising will be a single item. Digital commodities might come as close to getting something for nothing as any mercantile utopiast has ever dreamed.

Also, the groundwork for public acceptance of a digital economy has already been laid. For decades, telecommunications media have been conditioning us to accept information services as equivalent to material products. Because our media have been inculcating in us an artificially iconocized reality, they have also conditioned us for purely virtual products that are absolutely divorced from the physical world. Commodity exchange will be increasingly in our heads.

THE PORTRAYAL OF "NORMAL" WEALTH IN THE MEDIA

Television sit-coms and serials, as well as many mainstream movies, depict "normal" families living in large expensive houses in good neighbourhoods. Even "working-class" TV families such as Roseanne seem to live in solid-middle-class homes. The media present a world that most of their audience can only dream of. These video baubles of unobtainable existences are dangled in every household, where they exacerbate the immense thirst of the network audience for something better in life.

A recent statistic from the United States is telling. In *40 percent* of break-ins there, the intruders browsed through the refrigerator, and a significant number took the time to go through the family photo album. This figure indicates that thieves are like shoppers without money, and these days, more than ever, they are bankrupt shoppers acquiring the lifestyles they can't afford — not just icons of wealth and glamour but middle-class values.

Chapter 5

TELEDEMOCRACY:
Politics and Technology

TRANSHUMAN ECONOMIES

As the economy becomes global, Western governments will more and more fall into the role of trade-bloc managers, becoming like shadow corporations of dubious economic viability who increasingly look to business as a model of management and fiscal policy. In an age when international companies are beginning to assemble an electronic diaspora, geographically bound governments are at a disadvantage.

At the same time as corporations build larger and more complete files on their customers — files more complex and detailed than government records — governments will increasingly be in the position of having to rely on private companies to supply them with vital statistics on their own populations, statistics necessary to operate revenue-generating and social programs. Relative to corporations, governments will eventually be in an information-poor position.

Digital Marketing

Transhuman politics will be intimately linked with the digital economy, and global trade relations will probably be indexed by exhaustive product tracking. Once digitization is pervasive, marketing analysis might well become close to infallible, and total market saturation could become the norm. When precise methods of product-tracking are in place, production over-runs as well as warehouse gluts might become a thing of the past, and marketing will run more smoothly, at least for those within the loop. There will be less room for new businesses, however, and the cultural and digital markets will eventually become the only real area where innovation is possible. Information gathering and information management will become indispensable tools, and the market for customized search engines and corporate infobots, both computerized and human, will grow exponentially.

Digital Finance

As digital financing accelerates the speed of international transactions, money becomes more and more volatile, and increasingly abstract. At this moment, money is orbiting the Earth, funnelled through a ring of telecom satellites in an ethereal chain of electromagnetic pulses. These digital rings turn the Earth into a monetary Saturn, circled by a river of virtual currencies. Because financial markets follow the cycles of night and day, a tidal surge of digital cash follows the date line through the world's financial markets. Money, more divorced than ever from its material base of value relations in the physical world, has become pure information.

The accelerated speed of the digital financial markets was brought home by the largely computer-generated crash of October 19, 1987. Computers set to automatically sell off stocks below a certain price triggered a domino effect that ended with the New York Stock Exchange losing a staggering one-third of its value within a few hours. Unlike the crash of 1929, however — which also had its technological component, in telephones, ticker-tape machines and telegraphs — in this crash the self-regulating nature of modern financial markets soon re-established equilibrium, and no long-term economic depression set in. This time.

Transhuman Technology

The wave of technology that is almost upon us will not be just another manifestation of "progress" to be incorporated into society. It will alter the very basis of what it means to be human, and we cannot expect that economics, the social sciences and social systems such as democracy will survive as we know them. As we experience the impact of transhuman technology, political fragmentation will occur. Enclaves of extreme libertarianism, and even, perhaps, fascist pockets, will fill the temporary power vacuums that are created during the transhuman period. But eventually, barring catastrophe, the transhuman era will give way to an entirely new order.

At present, every political group, from neo-conservatives to libertarians and liberals, believes that technology offers some form of salvation. American leaders of all political stripes enlist technology as their ally, even though technology has no intrinsic social or political agenda, its ultimate function being to bring about our transformation. But, even if these various groups are deluded about what they believe to be the partisan nature of technology, their enthusiasm is essential, because, at this vulnerable and formative stage, transhuman technology needs all the help it can get. A devil's bargain with corporations is necessary in order to secure the vital private funding to finance research facilities that will eventually launch the posthuman era. The building of the transhuman era might well take place almost entirely in the realm of venture capital.

But make no mistake: posthuman technology will ultimately transform its corporate host, governments and all other extant forms of social organization. Until that point is reached, however, strong, democratic government with effective transnational laws will be instrumental in shaping the transhuman era, for the inequalities that will arise from the uneven distribution of extreme technologies will have to be controlled or else we will descend into chaos. When, finally, government as we know has been supplanted by whatever regulatory body replaces it, it must be left standing — useless, perhaps, but fully intact to the end.

DEMOCRACY

Democracy is in crisis, but not from external pressure; it is being questioned from within. Social-democratic liberalism, which has always operated on the belief that temporary suspensions of democracy are necessary to compensate for minority rights, is coming under attack, and democracy itself is breaking down precisely at the juncture between minority rights and majority rule that has defined liberal democracy for much of the twentieth century. Is it possible that this breakdown is, in part, the result of legislation being seen as dictated by the courts and not the ballot box, or is it being caused by populists using notions of direct democracy and referendums to undermine the powers of elected officials? The emotionalizing effect of the media, as well as the adversarial nature of jurisprudence and issue referendums, has psychologized minorities, and tragically their language is now one of victimization, restitution and culpability. As a result, democracy is losing its utilitarian justification, and the question of social justice has been reopened.

This psychologizing of minorities in particular, and the electorate in general, means that social issues, perceived injustices and their redressing are dealt with as a social *process* instead of as solutions. The result is that the current democratic evolution towards emancipation is, *de facto*, interminable, and this, in turn, limits the ability of any constitution or charter of rights to provide impartial and universal justice, because it cannot stand for more than a decade, let alone in perpetuity. This uncertainty cannot be alleviated by amending formulas. There is no longer a moral overview that relativizes social conflicts, and without a stable ethical instrument, government and society move onto unsteady ground.

The media have played a substantive role in accelerating this process. They have brought down European governments (they played a major role in the collapse of the Berlin Wall); they have influenced political discourse in North America; and they have amplified pluralism and nationalism globally, from Sarajevo to Quebec City. As a result, political conflict has, in the last decade, become cultural conflict. The flash point for this conflict is the struggle between liberal, social-democratic monoculture (i.e., American culture) and minority cultures, be they ethnic, religious or racial. The values of democratic monoculture have also become a specific target of "political correctness." But the "politically correct" movement is itself possibly a product of the emotionalization of politics by the media. It is important, also, to understand that the relationship between minorities and the "politically correct" is not necessarily intimate.

The pressure of minority agendas has created a political era in which jurisprudence and legislation shape each other more than they ever did before. Yet, having created the need for a more sophisticated political system, the West has not yet produced an alternative. Western civilization is finding its democratic basis being challenged, not by Marxist orthodoxies, but by international corporations and the influence of technology. We are in the peculiar position of being present at the birth of a new techno-political reality — a system that might ultimately supersede both democracy and communism — but of not knowing where or when it will arise. Certainly electronic polling, digital voting and electronic "town hall" meetings will be part of the new teledemocracy. But how the New Right, neo-conservatism and techno-libertarianism will fit in has yet to be determined. Whatever new system arises, it will be a bit of a political hodgepodge at first, with unconformable elements from older political affiliations co-habiting. It may well be that — invisibly — the new system is already up and running in some parts of the West, operating quietly, without a name and without anyone to identify it.

POLL-ITICS

Because television networks rely on audience ratings to determine the success of their broadcasts, they have become adroit pollsters and, by default, political. Anyone who makes public opinion his business is a *de facto* politician. It is only natural, then, that elected officials rely on electronic pollsters as much as do television executives. The confluence of their data sources — opinion polls and market surveys — parallels a deeper confluence of ideological manipulation, a subtle feedback effect that depends on audiences having their opinions sampled and reflected back to them instantaneously, faster than ballot-box results. What teledemocracy has done, with its instant electoral gratification, is to create the general impression that ballot-box democracy is slow and unresponsive. This frustration with the time-lag of democratic response is the reason why conservative think tanks are so enamoured of the idea of electronic voting.

Bill Moyers has described television as a "public mind." But television is also a public eye. It is an external sensory organ — outside of our bodies — yet as intimate as a secret ballot. The television industry constitutes a consensual, telecratic forum, and the triad of computers, television and electronic polling has created a new political reality. This is where television journalism, with its shoddy research, its ad hoc "experts" and its implicit biases, mistakes opinion for information. In this regard, television is the weak link in this political triad, and has considerable potential for damaging the truth, which is, after all, what democracy must be based on. McLuhan once said that rumours and gossip become the "real" world when they are accelerated by the electronic media. If this is the case, then the political "spin doctor" can rely on the gullibility of both newspapers and television to ensure that his or her client has the right "optics."

Market-research companies routinely format the order and phrasing of the questions on their surveys in order to manipulate the results. When the survey findings are published or broadcast, the figures are generally received by the public as objective, and thereby exert real influence by providing a bandwagon spin on the issues concerned. This process is perhaps the most sinister manipulation of teledemocracy. It is psychologically sophisticated (based on the same kind of psychological research that goes into high-end television and magazine advertising, for which expert psychologists are routinely consulted) and its goal is the building of an artificial consensus. The key component of this manipulation is the speed with which poll results can be disseminated, and then influence mass opinion. When the time for reflection and rumination is removed, polls end up favouring mass emotional responses over logical, reflective responses. The acceleration of this process by computers and telecommunication devices means that we, as audience and electorate, rarely get to consider an issue properly before we the electorate make a consensual decision. In this sense, therefore, the media, and those who can manipulate the media, make up our minds for us.

GLOBALISM AND THE NEW RIGHT

Most Western political ideologies, from secular liberalism to socialism, are the political grandchildren of Judaeo-Christianity, specifically its notion of "equality before God."

Liberal social democracy is a holy egalitarianism in which individual variation is subordinate to equality. Even Marxism, despite its fiercely anti-religious bias, is a product of the same basic Judaeo-Christian impulse. The premise of all these ideologies, from socialism to liberalism, is entrenched universality based on impartial justice.

Conversely, one of the most vital human resources is diversity, and diversity, of necessity, requires inequalities. The biological reality of human variation has always been a fly in the ointment of equality, as its arbitrary injustices contradict ideal values. Not only have diversity and its attendant inequalities been ignored by liberalism, despite its ostensibly meritocratic institutions, but they have also been levelled as much as possible. As a result, we have lost sight of the more valuable aspect of maximum diversity: only by having the widest spectrum of abilities, languages, cultures, sexualities and races can we have real learning. Cultural and political insights, even if manifested as conflict, are sparked only when differences rub against each other.

World media-culture globalism — as opposed to monoculture globalism — has opened up a new pluralism that the Right can no longer afford to ignore. A decade ago, this reality was recognized by the French New Right, which distinguished itself from the French conservative Right by embracing multiculturalism. Alain de Benoist, a spokesperson for the French New Right, defended pluralism in an interview, saying that "already on the international level, the major contradiction is no longer between Right and Left, liberalism and socialism, fascism and communism, 'totalitarianism' and 'democracy.' It is between those who want the world to be one-dimensional and those who support a plural world grounded in the diversity of cultures, between those who defend the cause of peoples and those who defend the rights and duties of the citizens who constitute them."

Because of this major policy shift by the New Right, the populist French Right has been forced to become, by default, a conservative Right, with its consequent emphasis on lowering immigration quotas and corporatizing government. Generally speaking, the Western populist Right, particularly its American branch, still identifies liberals as hucksters of disproportionate minority rights, and the liberals, in turn, are finding it difficult to explain the contradiction between policies such as affirmative-action hiring, whereby minority characteristics determine the choice of applicant, and "blind" justice, whereby all citizens are treated impartially, as equals. It is precisely at this meritocratic interface, where democracy slips into a subtle grey zone, that it is more and more vulnerable to manipulative lobbying by special interests, on the one hand, and media-influenced populist demands, on the other.

Neo-Conservatism and Techno-Libertarianism

It is no coincidence that neo-conservatism, in various forms, is on the rise at the same time as new technologies are being introduced. Burgeoning telephone networks, for example, became the nervous system for socialism's rise in Europe early in the twentieth century. The notions of empowerment and freedom inherent in personal computers and Internet access lend themselves readily to the desire for personal autonomy that is intrinsic to neo-conservative ideology. But the technological elite themselves — the futurists, the software designers, the transhumanists and

Xerox PARC executives — are almost uniformly libertarians. Their sense of technological empowerment is absolute. They are totally opposed to the idea of *any* government interference with the digital revolution or with personal use of the new media. In one sense, they are like super-conservatives, but they also embrace radical notions alien to conservatism. The libertarianism currently rising out of the Silicon Valleys of Western civilization is, like the French New Right, based on notions of pluralism. And it is this emphasis on diversity, seemingly inherent in new technologies, that gives Canada such a unique and poised position at the beginning of the transhuman era.

Canada's cultural-mosaic policy, which entrenches diversity, is more sophisticated than the American melting-pot policy, which encourages immigrants to submerge their identities into America's. Canada doesn't have the size to absorb immigrant cultures, and its liberalism is unique because it not only supports ethnicity, but encourages it. By acknowledging the solitude of other cultures, by encouraging their autonomy while at the same time trying to extend all the services of the secular/liberal state to them, Canada is, I would argue, among the most pluralistic countries in the world.

But again, in Canada, populism, a conductor for majority-rule intolerance, waits in the political wings, ever ready to take the stage. The eventual conflict may well turn out to be between city-states (the greatest unacknowledged political entities of the late twentieth century) and the populist hinterland. The multicultural cities of Toronto, Vancouver and Montreal, dependent on secular liberalism to operate, are becoming estranged from the conservative, unicultural rural electorate. The same values do not apply to both camps. The rural political scene has become populist because it adheres to more basic democratic

fundamentalism, a fundamentalism opposed to the techno-
cratic and unilateral actions sometimes taken by liberal governments, such as Trudeau's imposed bilingualism.

Liberalism, Multiculturalism and Power

Curiously, however, the same liberalism that seeks to sustain
the cultural mosaic is fundamentally incompatible with multiculturalism — primarily because culture is intrinsically
more powerful than politics. No political system born of a
specific culture can be used to administrate other cultures.
The European, Judaeo-Christian principle of secular liberalism is not the abstract, universal truth that its adherents in
the West think it is. In this sense, multiculturalism is the
enemy of liberalism, which is precisely the view of Alain de
Benoist and the French New Right. Whether or not this policy indicates a genuine belief of de Benoist's, or a cynical
strategy for gaining power, the logic of multicultural conservatism is faultless. Perhaps this explains why the French New
Right is also against "American imperialism." The French
New Right identifies America as the originator not only of a
pernicious monoculture, but of a liberalism that is destroying
democracy. Far from being the protector of cultural integrity,
the United States and most Western liberal democracies are,
according to the French New Right, committed to an ideological domination of the world.

The irony of a multiculturalist New Right being opposed to
American imperialism is not as surprising as it may at first seem.
The political ground is changing rapidly; with the end of Russian
Soviet socialism, the entire political spectrum has shifted to the
right. The most fascinating political development of the next

decade may be the convergence of techno-libertarianism with American neo-conservativism. This won't be the earnest techno-utopianism of Newt Gingrich, but a radical and sophisticated blend of technology and politics. America is the ideal breeding ground for such a symbiosis because American politics is both less intellectual and faster moving than European politics; mandates are more spontaneously derived in the United States.

Far Right groups in North America, such as the Christian Coalition, are proponents of what they call "radical democracy." Included in this notion is the concept of regional territories with self-determination. According to the Far Right, well-defined and autonomous regions could exist as affiliates of a republic, each of them having its own cultural mandate. The American New Right is already pushing education in this direction. Freed of state control, education would be able to transmit the values of ethnic and religious groups without the meddling of egalitarian liberalism. Paradoxically, this loose affiliation of ethnically determined, autonomous regions fits neatly with liberalism's emphasis on multiculturalism *and* libertarian concepts of "free ports." America might well evolve into a republic of ethnocultural territories, each with legislative autonomy. The liberal-democratic state may give way to a neo-republic composed of radical-democratic states.

The ultimate question will be how military power is vested. The concentration of military power in the hands of liberal democracies will not be given up easily, and the autonomous republics may turn out to be little more than freehold ghettos. But if power devolves to these pluralistic states, then a truly enforceable international law would be necessary. The contingency of newly fragmented national states may turn out to be a greater incentive for establishing international law, and the concomitant enforcement of the inviolability of borders, than any global monoculture.

THE POLITICS OF GENDER AND BIOETHICS

As technology increasingly intervenes in issues of gender and bioethics, they are drifting out of their political categories. Bioethics and gender issues are beginning to be perceived as having no innate political allegiances within the conventional continuum of Left and Right.

The definition of human liberties can be located within the traditional polarities of liberal and conservative politics, wherein the link between personal freedoms, such as the ability to travel freely or to own property, and their economic consequences are easily determined. But, when it comes to cultural liberties, such as freedom of religion, or biological liberties, such as the right to change sex, then the conventional ascriptions of political valence become more ambiguous, if not irrelevant.

It is possible, for example, to be a right-wing transvestite, just as it is possible to be a socialist anti-abortionist. That is why it is wrong-headed, and possibly dangerous, to allow any political interest, Left or Right, to politicize bioethics or gender issues. (The biological freedom of citizens must be entrenched.) Neo-conservatives, for example, have recently taken positions on many issues of gender and bioethics, positions they see as upholding "family values." But the "family" itself is in transition, and neo-conservatives run the risk of losing credibility, not only because society at large is depoliticizing gender and bioethics, but also because biotechnology is engendering so many changes, so quickly, that determining political positions within the rapidly evolving bioethical arena will be pointless.

POLITICAL CORRECTNESS

The very same ideological fluidity that is redefining the Right is also visiting the Left. Everything, from green politics to eco-terrorism, to animal rights, to political correctness, has become identified with the New Left. Additionally, none of these groups wants to commit to a single ideological platform because doing so might limit political flexibility.

The "political correctness" movement is getting the most media attention, though neither its adherents nor its detractors seem to have a clear idea of what constitutes political correctness. Certainly it is in part a product of the media, specifically television, which has retrieved, not just simmering nationalism, but age-old injustices and past wrongs. The psychological basis of political correctness appears to those outside its ideology to be the deep and unappeasable rage of the victim. This rage is quite different from the earnest protest of the late sixties, and its apparent toxic patina is understandably repugnant to most observers. In turn, the politically correct themselves view this repugnance as a rejection of their beliefs. Because response and counter-response to the ideology are so out of synch, no useful dialogue can be established. The mass-media audience of liberal-democratic monoculture is emotionally sophisticated but postliterate, whereas the overtly literate politically correct are stigmatized by their unacknowledged emotionalism.

Historical pluralism, a product of television, means that history can now revisit us. With it come the battles for emancipation that many in the West had thought were resolved. Without the current historical resurgence, political correctness would be completely incomprehensible to us in the West. (The resurrection of issues that had seemingly attained their political resolution decades ago is a symptom of the deep, sometimes justifiable, rage of the "politically correct.") Political correctness is largely a psychological movement, fuelled by the same media-induced emotionalism that is in evidence on afternoon TV talk shows — because they are unconscious of their hostility, the "politically correct" appear to brook no rebuttals. And this is what makes political correctness dangerous in an age when logic and due process are compromised by postliterate primitivism.

The frequent refusal of the politically correct to engage their foes in political discourse, as exemplified by some of Foucault's grandiose and self-righteous public pronouncements, is a type of McCarthyism of the Left. Opposing views are censored — university professors are shouted down, curators are stalked and harassed — in what is tantamount to a new inquisition, where self-appointed commissars determine whether university instructors will keep or lose their jobs, whether museums and art galleries will mount certain exhibitions, whether theatrical productions will be boycotted, or whether certain films or books and ideas will be taught or distributed, seen or read. Unfortunately for their own agenda, those who censure the ideology of their political foes also deprive themselves of an understanding of their foes' strategies. In the long run, this is political suicide.

Chapter 6

LOGO SAPIENS:
Language and Literature

LANGUAGE AND TECHNOLOGY

As Marshall McLuhan pointed out, most technology comes from language, and language itself was one of our first technologies. Language is also a living technology of consciousness. Language is hard-wired into our brains; it is part of our bodies, our vocal chords and mouths — part of us that is both old and strange. Our species has co-evolved with language, though the evolution of language sometimes seems to have its own agenda. At the same time, language is quite futuristic because it is an easily acquired mental software that allows humans to communicate, and its interface with us is practically seamless — even if the muscular paroxysms of language are not completely natural for primates. Language is as abstract and recombinant as any mathematics or digital code. From a finite series of characters and terms, an infinite number of sentences can be constructed.

Language is also a powerful, abstract, cognitive amplification system. Some researchers, such as the controversial

Julian Jaynes, have speculated that language sparked human consciousness. Certainly, as the neuro-philosopher Daniel C. Dennett has pointed out, an "externalized" logical system was quite a benefit for early humans. Dennett argues that what we refer to today as "interior monologue" was a very important function of early language, just as important as communication. With rumination, early humans could objectify their individual plans and ideas, and were consequently better able to manipulate them effectively. It follows that language is a sort of cognitive prosthesis that allows humans to amplify their actions in the world by externalizing their thinking.

The Power of Unnatural Order

The idiomatic expression "What's your handle?" reveals a great deal about how we use language to manipulate, not just concepts, but the physical world as well. A name allows us to get "hold" of a person or object because, when things are in categories, they can be operated on independently of their natural relations. At the time that humans first acquired language technology, it enhanced our ability to identify and collect natural objects, such as stones, fur and bones, with a view to their usefulness as tools, a use outside that which nature had intended for them. Humans derived both power and knowledge by altering the original order of nature, and we began to surround ourselves with artificial objects; woven clothing, metal tools and stone buildings. These artifacts were the progeny of language. Language, using human labour, built itself a physical vocabulary from these fabricated objects within the material space of the world. It is this vocabulary — our first, artificial environment — that allowed the meta-syntax of culture to be articulated. Not only is human consciousness perhaps a direct consequence of language, it is the result of a cognitive symbiosis with language.

Writing

Language introduced us, as a species, to the prosthetic cognitive tools of metaphor, analogy and comparison. Facts and observations could be taken from one context and inserted into a new one. These abstract juxtapositions became the engine of technology. Just as computers are accelerating and mutating our culture, so did written language, when it appeared in Sumer, accelerate and mutate the culture into which it emerged. Also, for the first time, writing allowed us to record conscious experiences and transmit them across time and space to distant readers.

We already had a good deal of experience delegating intelligence to language before the advent of writing, but the technology of writing sped up the effects of language on consciousness. For example, written language could be edited to artificially heighten the intelligence of texts. Writing completed the process of externalization that spoken language started. It was a thought amplifier that gave us the time to get it right. No human could think up a novel improvisationally without building it up from smaller bits.

Because language is so ubiquitous, we don't realize how much control we have delegated to it. Language and its operations may well make up most of human consciousness. If so, then true "voice recognition" (where the full range of human nuance and connotation, not to mention mumbling and slurring, is understood) in computers and automatic telephone operators will be equivalent to a Turing Test. (Allen Turing was a mathematician who gave his name to a test for artificial intelligence. This test is considered one of the best proofs of conscious awareness in a computer. It consists of a human in one room with a keyboard link to another room. The human isn't told whether he is communicating with a computer or with a human. If, after several minutes of dialogue, he still can't tell which is communicating in response, then the computer is, for all intents and purposes, conscious, and this means that artificial intelligence has been achieved.) Linguistic ability and consciousness may turn out to be more intimate than had been hitherto presumed. If such is the case, this is bad news for telephone companies, because practical voice recognition is still a long way off.

Visible Language

Human consciousness has a primal level at which every object that makes up our world consists of words in the shape of that object. This arrangement, a kind of projected, person-ificational literalism, may seem crude, but it has been corrob-orated by two very different phenomena. Under the influence of specific hallucinogenic drugs, particularly dimethyltrypta-mine, individuals report seeing the objects around them as being composed of the names of those objects. A cat, for example, would appear as a writhing, cat-shaped conglomer-ation of synonyms and associations for "cat," such as "kitty," "pussy," "meow," "tail," "ears," "claws," and "feline." These test individuals say that not only do they see the objects around them as being made of self-descriptive words, they also hear voices pronouncing and singing out the same words. The concreteness of this phenomenon seems to go well beyond association.

These "visible language" episodes could be dismissed as an idiosyncratic symptom of dimethyltryptamine intoxication (often invariant from subject to subject) were it not for another, separate confirmation. In psycholinguistics there is a well-known word-identification dyslexia that can be induced in practically anyone. You can duplicate this experiment at home with coloured markers and paper. If the word "red" is written in bright green ink, it causes some confusion when the subject is asked to name the colour the word is made of, that is, not the colour it names. This difficulty is exacerbated when the colour the subject is asked to identify is not only different from the name of the colour it forms, but the same as the named colour of the (also contrarily coloured) word next to it. For example, if the word "red" is written in green ink on a white sheet of paper, and then, just below it, the word "blue" is written in red ink, it is very difficult for most people to name without hesitation the colour that the word "blue" is written in. What is most telling about this interference is that the effect totally disappears when the differently coloured words are the names of familiar objects rather than the names of colours. (Thus, we expect a certain level of literalness in language and, if the literalness is contradicted, confusion sets in.)

These two examples of visual literalism are an excellent window into the insidious and almost total domination of our vision by language. It appears that our world is *made* of language, a living description of itself. To achieve absolution from this deeply ingrained crisis of naming (if absolution is what we seek), we would have to deliberately attain a state of complete visual anomia. This namelessness would be the product of a phenomenal labour of consciousness. I would venture that any spiritual or philosophical discipline which purports to attain such a condition will become increasingly palliative as long as language continues its influence over human perception.

LANGUAGE AS DOWNLOADING CONSCIOUSNESS

Semioticians have made much of what they term the "illusory transparency" of language. In their view, not only is language so utterly subjective as to be opaque, but it has become a "commodity fetish" whose economy is based on the delivery of meaning as a product. They also claim that the author, as a "privileged" producer of meaning, is a fallacious notion, and that the subjectivity of an individual reader's response denies any real communication of meaning between author and reader. (It has always struck me as somewhat ironic that semioticians and deconstructionists publish their work in the very medium which they decry.)

At the opposite extreme from the semioticians is Claude Shannon, a communication theorist. Shannon believes not only that language communicates messages, but that the theory of thermodynamics applies to language. Because of entropy (the third law of thermodynamics regarding the universal tendency of things to run down), he says, a message inevitably loses a small quantum of information any time it is communicated. In Shannon's theory, not only is language completely transparent, but it can be quantized.

I lean towards Claude Shannon's theory, but not because I deny the semiotic subjectivity of language. In the end, I believe we do communicate meaning. I think there is something wondrous about transferring thoughts and moods from one human to another through a series of abstract symbols. I have also come to believe that whatever shreds of consciousness — of being — that are "downloaded" into literature are transmitted whole and silently across time to the reader.

Reading as Downloading

Consciousness spawns consciousness; it rubs off against things. Perhaps consciousness is much more transferable than we had thought. If the ability to understand and use language embodies consciousness, then consciousness may be, as Daniel C. Dennett would have it, simpler than neuroscientists have made it out to be. What we want out of reading is to have someone else's consciousness rub off on us. Reading literature is like a prototype for downloading another consciousness into your own. It is not about commodity fetishism or the hopelessly subjective realm of the reader, nor is meaning bound to an economy of authority. Human languages, our common systems of reference, allow consciousness, in an unlikely but strangely efficacious manner, to be communicated, by what might be described, for lack of a better term, as a sort of manual telepathy between two humans. Significant levels of consciousness do inhabit literary texts, enough for the reader to get a virtual experience of another conscious human's existence from inside that existence. As long as sentient, conscious readers are around to reanimate them, literary texts do contain fragments of human consciousness.

LITERATURE AS ARTIFICIAL INTELLIGENCE

Art transforms the artist because of the exigencies of creation. A writer's work drives her. The demands of a text, if
the writer is truly dedicated to it, take the writer into areas
she would not normally explore. In the course of creation,
be it of a work of literature, or even of a series of sculptures
or paintings, the problems that arise out of the project's
necessities can become as important and demanding as the
project itself. In this way, the logistics of a creation influence
the artist so that she has to change, transform, in order to
accommodate the demands of the work. When she finally
arrives at the end of the work, a product of its own idiosyncratic criteria, it will be as different from her original
notions as she is from the person she was when she started
it. To a certain extent, artists' work defines and changes
them; it is an engine of their self-transformation. It is in this
sense, as an external, synthetic force, that art becomes a
form of artificial intelligence.

Random Composition and Computer-Assisted Literature

If the influence of writing on the writer is equivalent to a
form of artificial intelligence, then techniques which
heighten the influence of language on the text also support
this process. Early in the twentieth century, the Dadaist
poet Tristan Tzara experimented with a new technique of
literary composition that he called "cut-ups." By cutting
written pages into fragments and then recombining those
fragments arbitrarily, Tzara developed a random (aleatoric)
literary method of great efficacy. William Burroughs used

his own cut-up techniques, taking pages of his work, cutting and shuffling them, and then writing out the juxtapositions that occurred by chance. The introduction of the random, as a sort of irruption into the work, was treated with some oracular reverence by Burroughs. On the other hand, there *is* something almost magical about the influence of significant random events on our personal lives. Aleatoric literary techniques are almost a microcosm of the effects of random mutation on evolution, which is indispensable and profound.

The importance of random techniques of composition is that they mimic the impersonal, substitutive machinations of language itself. They harness the recombinant, artificial intelligence at the heart of language. It is supposed that our "personality," what we have to say in words, is prefigured by language, both in the way we communicate our thoughts and in the way we develop as individuals. By using a random technique, writers harness chance to create new meanings that bootstrap them out of the very ruts of habitual thought that language sometimes consigns them to. The kind of literary approach that accepts and includes the intrusion of aleatoric compositions has a significant advantage, which is its special humility, its willingness to accept the "alien," and this might well be a very central component of writers' new relation to their increasingly intelligent word processors, their digital "apprentices."

COMPUTERS AND WRITING

Computers are not only digital and binary, but also muta-genic. They transform whatever work is being done with them because they permit changes to be made more easily. Word processing has amply demonstrated how computers speed up and facilitate the alteration of documents. The ease with which manuscript changes can be made — renaming a character throughout a novel without having to retype hundreds of pages — is a good example. The *curriculum vitae* is another example, and is possibly the most ubiquitous of all word-processed documents. It is common practice for job applicants to weight their CVs in order to highlight the skills they need for a particular position. They can also customize their CVs visually to ape the typographic style of the company to which they are applying for work. Because all these changes are almost effortless once the original data have been entered into the computer, the ability to alter, to mutate the original document is enhanced.

When creation is easier, when the distance between an author and her final text is narrowed, the writer (or, for that matter, the composer or visual artist) is freer to invent, to imagine, to play. This freedom is the second characteristic of computers, and it elevates the computer to more than a tool, since its delibility allows the writer to endlessly alter her products. There is word-processing software available right now that takes a written work, reconfigures it, and prints out new combinations that imitate the author's style and yet also challenge her by creating unexpected permutations. These juxtapositions are tantamount to a deep rethinking of the author's work. It seems to me that the computer and the author will develop an increasingly symbiotic relationship. Rather than wringing our hands about these changes to the arts, I think we should be waiting on the edge of our seats for what will shortly be emerging.

COMPUTER-ASSISTED LITERATURE

After all, many publishers used computer programs — highly specialized, but unsophisticated algorithms, without the remotest possibility of self-awareness — to routinely produce both literature, and literary criticism, indistinguishable from the human product. Not just formularised garbage, either; on several occasions I'd been deeply affected by works which I'd later discovered had been cranked out by unthinking software.

— from *Axiomatic* by Greg Egan

Hypertext

Several novelists have ventured into electronic publishing over the past decade. Besides having their books available on-line, they have also configured their texts to include hypertext links. (Underlined words can be clicked on to gain entry into related texts, images or other parts of the narrative.) Hypertext novelists claim that this process, a sort of electronic footnoting, revolutionizes the way readers experience novels. Certainly hypertext novels have spun off an alternative narrative genre in conventionally published books. For example, R. L. Stine, a writer of young-adult fiction, brought out a line of books in which various pages linked to new endings. Because readers lose interest in limited threads of association fairly quickly (like the limited choices of alternative narratives in current video games), I suspect that hypertext novels may eventually turn out to be a literary dead end, though computer-assisted literature *is* advancing in other areas.

Permutative Programs

An artist's critical objectivity is crucial to her success, but producing enough material to feed that objectivity is even more crucial. What artists do best is make aesthetic judgments within an array of possibilities. The greatest composers, painters, writers and sculptors produce dozens of prototypes either physically or in their imaginations and, after scanning the contenders, choose the correct one.

For the artist, making the right choice is difficult, particularly after she has had to create the possibilities from among which she will choose. This is where computers, using aleatoric and "evolutionary" software, will become indispensable, because computers are adept at mindlessly churning out variations on possible themes. The artist will be freed to exercise her talent for discerning beauty and meaning from an array of possibilities.

There is already an underground market in computer-assisted-literature software. Pre-eminent among these are the "cut-up" systems such as Babble! (Korenthal, 91) that have rudimentary author-syntax recognition features. I have personally discovered the peculiar delights of some of these programs, using my own work as input. One program did a statistical analysis of my style and then recombined it in a style similar to my own, but in completely novel combinations. It was chilling, eerie and, at the same time, curiously exhilarating. The writing that the program produced was *much* more than a cut-up, or purely random shuffling. The following is an example:

> How many times, in the quietness of an ice-age darkness, have you told me that winter is the light in the kitchen, the icicle that cut me? Birds were visible across the months of sunlight, holding their neutral temperature as if they were the solutions of sado-masochistic algorithms that had flourished long ago on the moon. Her face is a woodlot, containing empty floating islands sculpted by the city she had left forever. She sang with her back to the open door, the door that had blown open four times in the synthetic darkness. Later on, in the kitchen, she erased their personal memories.

By delegating some control of the writing to computers, which will be increasingly qualified to handle such material, the writer will become liberated. The choices that she will make within the alternatives that the computer produces will become the central authorial contribution to the process. Because both language and the computer have their own programs, authorial style might eventually become the executive "software" that controls the programs of both language and the computer.

The only victim of this marriage of artist and computer will be human hubris and false pride. We need real humility to take advantage of our new instruments, particularly in the face of sceptical Luddites who would have us step back from the brink. As programs become more intelligent, and computer-assisted art becomes more symbiotic, then profoundly new art forms may arise. The age of the first *real* computer literature may soon be upon us.

COMPUTER-ASSISTED ART

The constraints placed on the production of art by the various media that interpose themselves between an artist's idea and its execution are not necessarily a formative discipline that weeds out the unmotivated artists. They may simply be pointless barriers, distractions that, once dispensed with by computer-assisted composition, will fall away like the shed skin of a snake.

The Eventual Emergence of "Natural" Genius

When you whistle a tune into a computer and ask it to score the melody for two violins, have it play back the score, and then, after listening, ask it to change the key from, say, D to G, and add a new piano line, which you whistle over the violins, have that played back to listen for mistakes, and then, finally, have the whole thing transcribed into hard copy to be faxed to your agent in Tokyo; when, as you are hiking through the mountains, you suddenly realize that the ending of a chapter of your novel would be better if you added a new scene, and you use your celluar phone to call your computer at home and discuss text changes with it while your computer, in word-processing mode, makes additional, helpful editorial suggestions (much as if it collaborated on the writing) and then reads the piece back to you in marvellously modulated con-versational English (or French or Cantonese); when your purest, most spontaneous flashes of insight and creativity are effortlessly translated into enhanced music, sculpture and prose, you will be one of a new breed of artists.

New technologies and capabilities will engender new artistic disciplines, and certainly enrich current ones. Rather than their leading to superficial work, I think these enhance-ments will assist in the production of deeper and more engaging creations. At the same time, proprietary notions of authorship and "individuality" will be challenged by artists' collectives and new methods of creation. I don't think these productions will be sterile; they will not be "machine art," as uncomformable with the human spirit as today's synthetic implants are with the body, but rather the products of a transparent technology that facilitates and enhances the work of art without interposing itself. Purely natural artists, unhampered by menial cognitive labour — undisciplined, in the old sense — will arise, and these impulsive, wilful geniuses will create new worlds.

COMPUTERS, LITERACY AND COMPUTER-ASSISTED LITERATURE

At present there are no hard data supporting the notion that computers are responsible for rising levels of illiteracy, or, indeed, that levels of illiteracy are rising at all. I think that the current debate about the effect of computers on literacy is premature. Serviceable voice recognition, when computers are able to convert spoken sentences directly into type and then read them back, will have a much larger, possibly negative, impact on literacy. Writing skills will definitively be affected when PCs are able to take dictation. This advancement, along with more sophisticated "spell-check" and "grammar-consulting" programs, will allow illiterate individuals to write perfectly spelled, grammatically correct correspondence, even if they are incapable of signing their own names. PCs with voice recognition will become scribes for the illiterate. Furthermore, you will not even need to buy a computer. You might be able to dictate your message into a terminal, perhaps one located at a variety store or newsstand, have your message read back to you (with editorial suggestions), and then make the changes appropriate for your intended recipient. The finished message could be sent by conventional surface mail, FAX or e-mail.

The scenario I've sketched out above may remain hypothetical, but it is possible that, when voice recognition eventually becomes commonplace, literacy may become redundant, gradually undergoing devolution into an unobtainable skill. Literacy might one day be regarded with the same awe that we reserve for the feats of Olympic athletes or the abilities of memory prodigies who are able to recite large sections of the Bible by heart. Reading and writing may become the clannish capabilities of an elite whose members recognize one another by their esoteric abilities, like the execution of a Freemason's handshake. In short, things we today take for granted about literacy might, in the future, assume almost magical dimensions.

It is a general rule of technological progress that, as human skills are superseded by machines that are stronger, faster, and now smarter, then the skills these machines replace become anachronisms that are practised as recreational activities.

Horse-riding used to be our dominant means of transportation, now it is almost purely recreational. Cognitive skills are no exception to this rule of obsolescence. When printing presses made books available to everyone, then the ability to memorize texts became redundant, practised mainly as a recreation by a few scholars.

Those who worry about how electronic books and interactive media will challenge literacy *should* be concerned, but it's possible that their focus is at the wrong end of the reader/writer relationship. I think that the effect computers have on writers will become the contentious issue, and that the eventual struggle for authorial primacy between computer text generators and writers will be the unexpected challenge that literature will have to face. This battle will be waged in the writers' heads, not on readers' laps. I think that the impact of voice recognition will be of secondary importance relative to the change in literature that will be wrought as writers begin to use computers as digital apprentices. Word processing, with grammatical and stylistic software systems, will reach such a level of sophistication that no writer will be able to do without them, lest she lose her advantage over other writers.

Meanwhile, critics of computer-assisted literature will claim that nothing can replace the unique human writer, and, furthermore, that accepting the poisoned apple of computer-assisted literature is "cheating." This is where their logic fully collapses, because we humans have always "cheated" with language.

Is using a thesaurus cheating? Isn't being influenced by other writers a sort of cheating, or worse? And, above and beyond both language and writing, aren't our personal identities a form of cheating? After all, we *are* complexes of borrowed and learned behaviours and gestures, not to mention societal conditioning. These influences seek expression within an author's texts as urgently as does her unique voice.

Traditionally, writers have been regarded as singular artists who produce original works. Certainly the true innovators of literature have risen well above cliché, and originality is the highest value in art, but, at root any work of literature is a collage of concepts, phrases and styles. All books consist of a combination of influences and concepts. There never was, nor ever will be, an *entirely* original literary work.

The ethical question of an author's proprietary rights and originality in terms of computer-assisted literature must also be asked in relation to the ownership of language. Whatever we claim to be "our own" or "original" in our use of a collective system of reference — language — is suspect. To delegate creative processing to a computer is not to say that "I" didn't do the writing. It may be that the artificial line we have drawn between "self" and "not self" will become irrelevant in a future in which "self" as we know it transforms into something unrecognizable.

But this incipient revolution will not be for everyone. True, a third of all North American homes have computers, but the other two-thirds currently without computers may never be able to afford them and may never want them. Ten years ago, pundits predicted that, as computer chips got smaller and cheaper, the price of computers would plummet. By the mid-nineties, they said, powerful home computers would cost less than $500. As anyone who has recently purchased a new computer knows, the price for recent models is gradually rising. We are constantly hearing from digital Utopians how electronic technology will democratize society, making the have-nots into the information rich. We hear how previously marginalized members of society will gain a voice. Certainly voice recognition will allow illiterates to write, but the economically disadvantaged will continue to have neither the time nor the inclination to take advantage of information technology the way the advantaged do. The equipment expenses and the levels of education necessary to enter the "digital revolution" almost certainly ensure that the poor are excluded from its highest levels, and this will become a social issue we all must address.

JOURNALISM AND INFORMATION

This is the golden age of journalism. The journalistic success of novelists such as Norman Mailer in the sixties and seventies paved the way for journalism's complete domination not only of media, but also of literature. Hollywood's emphasis on narrative scripts, coupled with the conversational style of gonzo journalism developed in the seventies and eighties, has infiltrated late-twentieth-century media culture.

The television journalist is at the top of the writing food chain. Television journalism, even though it is geared to a visual medium, sets the standard for almost all other types of writing. Most publishing houses today favour short, lucid sentences that are "front-end loaded." The content or style of a sentence must always be secondary to its accessibility; nothing can stand in the way of "readability." The universally despised "sound byte" is the direct symptom of this policy.

The fact that the media are partially if not wholly responsible for our current predicament of consensual autocracy, with its ubiquitous, commercialized social propaganda, hasn't detracted from the immense fascination they hold. The audience is still credulous, even if a little sceptical. In fact, it is the media's success in the face of general audience cynicism that's truly remarkable. We may not believe the messenger, but we still buy his wares.

What *is* pernicious, however, about the dominance of journalism in both literature and the media is the increasing paucity of information it delivers. In an age when we are being told that we suffer from "information overload," we are, in actuality, less informed than ever before. Most media journalists, particularly in television, rely on extremely deficient research. Their system of gathering information, based on a network of "credible sources," is susceptible to bias and manipulation. Possibly journalists are not completely at fault, since the time necessary for deep research is not available to them. Nevertheless, the result is similar: shallow coverage and perennial sources — the same "'experts,'" regardless of their real qualifications, are brought before the evening-news cameras again and again.

As well, in order to become "accessible," the media have debased (i.e. "dumbed down") their vocabularies and, in a sort of unilateral condescension, have decided that information has to be delivered in a form that is "understandable" or "interesting" to an audience that they arrogantly regard as a mass of simpletons who are unable to appreciate in-depth or intelligent treatments of complex issues. A symptom of the lack of independent research in news departments — of newspapers, radio and television — is the high degree of similarity between their reports. From channel to channel, medium to medium, news has become generic, in both the order of the stories and the content of the reports.

This pandering to a hypothetical "average" audience, composed of theoretical dullards, has debased journalism. News, competing with a variety of other entertainments for ratings and readers, has had to avoid information and plunge into the realm of opinion, gossip and spectacle.

When the cold war ended in 1989, I looked forward to the possibility that the media might focus their attention on what I considered to be an immense and threatening problem: mega-pollution — namely, the twice-daily dumping of New York's garbage in the Atlantic Ocean. This huge undertaking, on the scale of giant engineering projects, has turned the Atlantic Ocean at the horse latitudes into a floating delta of Javex bottles from horizon to horizon. Well, finally, I thought, something will be done now, and none too soon. But, years passed and the issue wasn't even mentioned in the news. Even Greenpeace ignored it, or seemed to. But, then, in the self-fulfilling prophetic world of media journalism, sea-fill garbage just wasn't sexy. And if it isn't interesting, it isn't news, and it won't get covered, regardless of its importance.

ORIGINALITY IN THE MEDIA

We in the West live in a paradoxical culture. Originality is scarce, yet at the same time it is the only source of profit for mass entertainment. "New" ideas make money. But not *too* new. As a society, particularly in terms of our mass entertainment, we seem to mistrust the original, the eccentric, and we tolerate it less each decade. The roots of our fear of originality reach deep into the beginning of our century.

At the dawn of the twentieth century, the family was the basic unit of production. A 1910 family, with tasks divided along gender lines, could make furniture, clothing, toys; raise a vegetable crop; and do light construction. Over the course of the twentieth century, the family has been transformed from a productive unit into a purely consumptive one. The family, and consequently our entire society, has become alienated from the origin and means of production much more profoundly than Marx had ever dreamed. For us, everything is fabricated elsewhere. This process, which began with commodities such as appliances, toys, clothing and food, eventually extended itself to culture. But this did not happen until the forties and fifties, and the process of cultural commodification wasn't complete until the late eighties.

The commodification of culture is one explanation for the marginalization of the avant-garde. Another is that extreme originality is no longer trusted and is viewed as pathological. Avant-garde artists such as Picasso and Virginia Woolf, who could be appreciated by mass culture in the thirties, would not even make the entertainment sections of newspapers, were they starting out today.

Issues of Appropriation

The prodigious hunger of the mass-entertainment media for new content has resulted in a media clear-cut zone. On the edge of this zone stand ethnic and aboriginal cultures that look increasingly inviting to the mass media. As any kind of moderate originality becomes a potential source of lucrative material, the inevitable use of marginal cultures has led to issues of appropriation. But the question of cultural appropriation, especially in literature, is really the question of originality in a different guise. A literary appropriation of indigenous mythology is merely a symptom of a larger appropriativeness. The cultural industry has ceased to produce, and has undergone the same transformation from producer to consumer that the Western family has over the course of the twentieth century. The media is now a net consumer of culture. In this cultural climate, it is becoming harder to create new worlds. Originality, which is the highest value of art and literature, is so rare that it is not recognized when encountered, and barely trusted when recognized.

LITERATURE'S SLIDE INTO PRE-MODERNISM

Perhaps one of the most insidious effects of the mass-entertainment media has arisen from the privileging of the eye over the ear. We have a general impatience with complexity, because the visual media, such as television and movies, do not need as much interpretation as do the print media.

At the same time, as McLuhan pointed out, there has been a retrieval of orality, and today, more than ever, a fast tongue is prized. The days of the "strong, silent type" seem to be long gone. Certainly our visually biased, oral culture permeates all contemporary media. Which may be the reason why popular culture appears to find mime artists both quaint and ludicrous: people who do not talk are disadvantaged. Our verbal bias, however, is limited to vernacular forms: "street talk," the stand-up comic or the satiric put-down. Oral culture rejects rhetoric and avoids complex or educated discourse. This may explain why one strain of contemporary novels, such as those that emerge from the Gordon Lish school (a New York writing school that produced many contemporary novelists), have embraced both minimalism and elements of confessional journalism. Mainstream literature is retrieving even earlier forms, and as nostalgia for Victorianism gains momentum, even the minimalist novels of the late 1980s are being pushed aside by the ornamental historical tomes of neo-Victorian literature, such as the novels of A.S. Byatt.

If this literary recidivism is a failure of progress in the arts, and it certainly does resemble one, there are other factors that have influenced its decline. One of the traditional watchdogs of the "new" has been the avant-garde, whose stalwart presence throughout most of the twentieth century served as an incentive to originality. But the avant-garde (lampooned by the visual media since the fifties) has failed, in part by being co-opted by the media, but primarily by marginalization. The failure of avant-garde literature is linked to the somewhat laudable defeat of deconstructionism in mainstream critical journalism (though there are some pockets of resistance in universities). At the same time, unfortunately, the collapse of the avant-garde in literature has opened the way for literature's slide into pre-modernism. The only exception to this slide has been post-modern writing, but that is really a sort of pop literature, acceptable because it confirms contemporary values.

At the time of this writing, the "literary novel" is enjoying huge popularity, with record high sales. As I mentioned, however, among current novels there is a large percentage of neo-Victorian, historical fictions that emphasize the "exotic." This stress on exotic or ethnic components in historical fiction is a function of the liberal classes, who are fuelling our contemporary literary renaissance with their vast purchasing power.

Their fascination with exotic cultures, with thinly veiled travelogues and histories, is a resurfacing of Victorian exoticism camouflaged as liberal emancipation.

Taken together, visual-dominated media, the failure of the avant-garde and the rise of neo-Victorian literature have tilted literature backwards, and created a conservative, somewhat materialistic literary ecology. I don't think that it would be an overstatement to say that it is unlikely that a manuscript by an unknown Gertrude Stein or James Joyce would be considered "marketable" by today's literary publishers.

PAGE AS SCREEN

A white page is a static, passive screen, but it is no less a screen than a television or a computer monitor. Screens have been with us for thousands of years. Our first screen was the papyrus scroll. (We have come full circle, for word processing has retrieved the scroll in an electronic form.) Our proclivity to view any blank space as a tablet or screen for our projected thoughts is natural to us, and probably derives from language. What has changed with the advent of the computer is the ability to use and reuse the same screen for different content, over and over, instead of just once, as in books. Computers, unlike paper, are infinitely delible. (The computer mimics vision in this way also; as is true in our visual field, various scenes can sequentially inhabit the same screen.)

In man-made environments, screens are ubiquitous. Signs are screens. Even walls and the surfaces of machines can become screens for printed messages. The urban surface is a continuous screen, or a series of overlapping screens, onto which representations are projected. Skin is a screen for tattoos. When it comes to representation, human consciousness is predicated on screens.

Advertising signs are screens that we cannot ignore because we are open to literal suggestion. For that reason, advertising messages are intrusive, impinging on our ability to concentrate, to maintain continuity. Signs keep changing the subject since we must constantly make choices, accepting one product while rejecting another (at least conceptually) as we look at the ads. Advertising catapults us into a field of equivocation and uncertainty; it dislocates us by interrupting our narrative continuity. The proliferation of eye-grabbing advertising, in terms of its increasing domination of our visual space, might be one of the main origins of the breakdown of narrative in the postmodern age.

LANGUAGE AS SCAFFOLD

Perhaps language has almost fulfilled its function as an intermediary stage between monkeys and gods. Language is the software that transfigured human minds and bred our technologies. Now it has brought us to a historic juncture. The potential for complete transcendence of our present condition is fast upon us, and it may be that a new language will spring up; in fact, it has probably already begun to develop, in some practical and everyday corner of our current technology. Language, at least as we now know it, may be left behind, an empty sign of the way we passed.

Chapter 7

DIGITAL APPRENTICES:
The Computer Era

COMPUTERS

By putting our physical bodies inside our extended nervous system, by means of electric media, we set up a dynamic by which all previous technologies that are mere extensions of hands and feet and teeth and bodily heat-controls — all such extensions of our bodies including cities — will be translated into information systems.

— Marshall McLuhan

The digital nature of computers distracts us, and consequently we confabulate mythologies about them and miss their invisible, yet essential, properties. Computers are cognitive amplifiers that augment thinking the same way that machinery amplifies muscle. They are also transparency devices that translate and transform data. They are mutative mechanisms; the very nature of their efficiency — their extraordinary speed and the subtle influence of their processing — mutates the information that we manipulate with them.

Computers have another marvellous quality: they are digital sponges, drawing the world into themselves as if they were made of some magic absorptive substance that soaks up information.

AT PLAY IN THE FIELD OF EQUIVALENCIES

Any operation that a computer undertakes is equivalent to any of its other operations. The emotional value that the user attaches to the documents and programs that he is manipulating have no such importance to the computer. This principle of equivalence permeates all the operations of the computer; the computer only facilitates the algorithmic manipulation of symbolic bits.

The flow of influence is not only in one direction. The ways in which a computer executes and processes the commands of its user influence the (display and) implementation of those commands. The computer's impartiality, its "non-values," are an ambient part of any user's interaction with a computer, and they eventually permeate the cognitive space of the operator, even if unconsciously. This impartiality is a cybernetic dispassion, and it can provoke a background of anxiety in the human operator, who, as all humans do, weights his actions emotionally with his investment of time, energy and thought. For us it is frustrating to lose a file that represents hours of work, or to have a system crash in the middle of a highly concentrated work session. Whereas, to the computer, five minutes of lost work is the same as five hours, and the data in a piece of personal correspondence is equally as important as the screen icon.

Not only does the impartiality at the heart of the computer subtly pervade the unconscious of its operators, but, on a deeper level, it parodies the processing equivalencies in our own cognitive system. All signals in the brain, regardless of their origin or destination, are merely impulses that are shunted along the endless complexities of neurological structures. The image of a rose, the feeling of a pinprick, the memory of a day at the beach — all are equivalent within the brain when they are reduced to neurochemical impulses.

By metaphorizing the deep reality of our own thought processes, the computer evokes an intuited realization that the world is, in all its aspects and in terms of our deep cognitive reality, equivalent to itself in all its parts. No part is more or less important than any other part, and every thing can be replaced by or traded with any other thing because all have equal representational value. In terms of cognition, this propensity is somewhat hellish for us, because humans use extremely relative, hierarchical systems of emotional attachments, judgments and ascriptions of relative valences to negotiate the world. For us, the world is a dynamic, involving and motivational sphere within which we can make real emotional investments, and this may explain why, when we first perceive computers, we find their monotonous consistency almost neurotic.

COMPUTERS AS COGNITIVE AMPLIFIERS

Computers are extensions of our minds — as you discover when you try to use someone else's computer. It is almost like looking inside that person's head. Other people often personalize their adjustable settings or they order their files in a system you find baffling. Probably their screen icons are different from yours. It is these character traits that make using another person's computer a vicarious experience, providing a sense of voyeurism similar to that of secretly leafing through someone else's personal diary.

At the same time, computers are more than repositories for our memories and plans; they stand alone. They are half tool, half entity. Think of your home and recall how you relate to various appliances, your emotional response to them. Think about your refrigerator, your television, your lawnmower. You may have an emotional bond to your car, but that is anthropomorphic projection. Now, think about your computer, think about how you'd feel if you lost all the information stored in its memory. It is almost unthinkable. We have a much higher level of investment in and personal identification with our computers because we have delegated some of our mental functions to them. Computers are more than helpers, though they are less than companions. They seem to have a low-grade entity charge, a charge that is qualitatively different from the way we sometimes personalize our machines.

Each new technology that humans adopt has the effect of amplifying our actions. Each new technology is a barrier removed between us and our ultimate freedom. As knives amplify and extend teeth and fingernails, as pliers amplify fingers, so do computers amplify our brains. Our identification with our computers marks the beginning of an incremental merging process whose end point will be a symbiosis of sorts. But this process, ultimately, is not going to be restricted to the private relationship between individuals and their PCs. The interconnectivity of the telecommunications matrix that we are all wired into ensures that the relationship will be social. We are collectively delegating vast amounts of cognition to computers, and we are increasing the load as fast as we can. We are already flowing into our machines, and human faculties, our memories and our creativity, are slipping into computers like fish slipping out of aquariums into lakes.

COMPUTERS AND THE EVOLUTION OF ELECTRONIC DEVICES

Electronic technology is evolving towards essentialization. When home stereo systems were first marketed in the 1960s, they were housed in large wooden cabinets the size of a small freezer. At first these systems were produced by a single company, but then, gradually, component-system manufacturers began to specialize in only speakers or amplifiers. The oversize stereo housing was dropped as a result, and the individual functions of the stereo system evolved into today's modular components. Today any company's speakers can be connected to any other company's amplifier and any other company's CD-player.

This same evolutionary pattern will be true for home computers, which are essentially home-entertainment, information-processing systems. Compared with recent laptops, the early PCs were huge. Throughout the eighties, computer manufacturers resisted the natural process of miniaturization that they were technologically capable of at the time. Computer consoles could have been a third the size they were. Perhaps marketing surveys didn't ask the right questions, and it would seem that historical comparison with home-entertainment systems didn't occur to anyone. The advent of flat, high-resolution screens and powerbooks has put an end to all that. Like the trend in stereos in the late sixties and early seventies, that for computers is clearly towards components, with separate manufacturers for keyboards, hard drives and monitors. The key factor will be interchangeability of components.

Another factor that has been holding back the evolution of the personal computer is the continuing, unholy wedding of the anachronistic electron-scan television screen to the computer. In terms of computers, cathode television is an obsolescent visual technology, and is antithetical to concentration and clear judgment, particularly in word processing. Using a cathode-ray television screen with a word processor is like using a steam engine to power a rocket, or a horse to pull a car. It is distracting and inefficient (not to mention dangerous) to stare down the barrel of an electron-scanning gun mounted twelve inches from your face. Enormous profits await the first company to produce an affordable stand-alone, fifteen-inch high-resolution flat colour screen that is universally adaptable.

Memory as Fat

Software has become very memory-intensive. The demand for more memory is insatiable. Microsoft Word has to be "spring-loaded," compressed onto seven double-density discs. Claris Works uses at least twenty megabytes of ROM and four of RAM. Windows 95 requires even more ROM, and sixteen megabytes of RAM. Bulk memory gives code writers more elbow room for the provisional, rushed programming that massive software systems like Windows 95 and Windows 98 need. If the power is there, they say, why bother editing code to make it more efficient? We have entered the decadent period of computer software. Without the discipline and incentive of limited memory space, code writers simply use bulk memory to compensate for ad hoc programming. Whatever happened to the elegant, memory-lean software of the early eighties — the MacWrites and the various share-ware games and simulations that could be loaded onto a single disc? Why, in this age of Mandelbrot sets, where a single algorithm can describe infinitely complex and beautiful worlds, are we stuck with such unwieldy, memory-hungry software behemoths?

Icons and Avatars

The collapse of the world into micro-space is facilitated, in part, by computer screens, which convert selected three-dimensional spaces into two dimensions. For example, instead of our having to shuffle papers on a desk, or go through a filing cabinet, the "windows" format allows us to manipulate virtual papers and files in a purely two-dimensional space. Computer screens are a reduction, a transubstantiation into virtuality. Icons also reduce the physical world into micro-space by shrinking the actual size of the depicted object or function. The filing cabinet becomes a small icon on the screen, as does the wastepaper basket. On the Internet, individuals are represented by "avatars," visual icons that, like cybermorphs, stand in for them in cyberspace. Icons and avatars are becoming heuristic signs that collapse meaning like ideographs or characters do. It is, after all, easy for us to reduce the world to abstract symbols; we've done it in the form of language for thousands of years.

What is different about computer icons is that their flatness is only temporary. In a sense we are already operating three-dimensional virtual realities on our computer screens. When you open more than one window, the first window is "behind" the new one, the way a sheet of paper is underneath another. Paper is nominatively treated as two-dimensional, as its thickness is negligible. However, paper does have a thickness, and that dimension is simulated in the — albeit thin — three-dimensional virtual reality of the computer screen. In other words, nominal three-dimensional realities are already commonplace to those who use Macintoshes or Windows.

Interfaces

There have been many science fiction stories written about the physical union of brains and computers. In the movie *Lawnmower Man,* the limp body-shell of the protagonist is left after his mind is literally swallowed by a computer. In *Johnny Mnemonic,* the protagonist has a "neural implant" that augments his own natural brain capacity. This kind of hyperbolic futurism, endemic to science fiction, overshadows the subtle interface between brain and computer that we already have. In one sense, there is no need to wire computers directly into our brains as we have adequate access to them through existing "interfaces:" the keyboard, mouse and screen.

Software, an often overlooked interface, is a virtual control panel inside a computer. Spanning two realms, it represents itself both to the operator, with screen icons and keyboard interfaces (so that the operator can use the software), and to the hardware, as machine instructions, mathematically specifying the exact operations for the hardware to perform. Software is more than the ghost in the machine; it is a bridge, like Jacob's ladder, between human perception and machine operations.

On the other hand, the interface between the computer and our nervous systems will nevertheless deepen — going from keyboard to joystick to mouse to touch-screens to data-glove to voice recognition. The end point of this evolution will be transparency, the complete biological integration of the computer: either the body swallowing the computer or the computer swallowing the body. Most likely both processes will occur, as they have already begun, incrementally and simultaneously.

DISPOSABLE INTELLIGENCE

Eventually our environments will become smarter and smarter as logic chips and microprocessors insinuate themselves into almost everything. Logic chips, which are really microcomputers, have already invaded a number of household appliances. My desktop printer, for example, a Macintosh StyleWriter, has a small logic chip in the ink cartridge (because some of the printing computations are delegated to the cartridge). When the cartridge is empty, it becomes a disposable brain. (Perhaps this is the leading edge of an evolution that will end up with artificial entities that have been programmed to possess human cognitive capabilities but are designed "soul-less" so that they are expendable.)

The instruction manual that came with the StyleWriter indicates that if the ink cartridge malfunctions — creating lines or linear gaps in the printout — you can remedy this malfunction by pressing two buttons simultaneously on the StyleWriter. This action sends a signal to the logic chip on the cartridge to "clear" it, like electro-convulsive therapy "clears" a depressed patient. Sometimes I entertain the fantasy that any printing malfunction of the microchip in the cartridge is a form of rudimentary self-expression, that the chip is a nascent artificial entity trying to communicate by modifying the printout. In short, the chip "gets ideas." And we respond by clearing its little brain so that it will be a mindless servant for the larger computer. Whenever I throw out my empty ink cartridges, I feel a little guilty about disposing of those little brains. What a loss. They could be the mind of a microbot.

Microprocessors represent a level of computation, a sort of low-grade intelligence, that is invading more and more of the previously "brainless" objects around us. If chips of ever-increasing sophistication are placed in more and more practical items — car radios, microwave ovens, automobiles, printers and cellular phones — our environments will gradually become sentient.

SELF-AWARE ENVIRONMENTS

A smart room, as envisaged by Alex Pentland of the Media Lab at the Massachusetts Institute of Technology, is a room in which microprocessors have been implanted in every appliance and every utility and communications device. They can all "talk" to one another via a network. But these micro-processors have a special advantage over their commercially available counterparts: not only are they connected with one another and with the rest of the house, they can also *see* and *hear,* using cameras and microphones. Because they are not passive devices that await instructions from a keyboard or a mouse, they represent a reversal of the ordinary interface priority which focuses on making it easier for humans to use a computer. In the smart room, the interface is biased towards the computers, making it easier for the computers to talk to humans — though the overall effect will still be to render the human/computer interface more transparent.

A smart room that had facial-recognition devices could tell when you were tired and would dim the lights, or automatically start the coffee maker. The microprocessors of a smart room could delegate computation to a cognitive net that would improve the responsiveness of the environment, literally anticipating the needs of the room's owner as it learns her habits. As she sat at her desk, the smart room's personal computer would turn itself on. The "smart" toaster would not only toast her bread perfectly, it would alert the automatic coffee maker to scan its memory files and determine if it was probable that she'd like coffee with her toast. The refrigerator, aware of its own contents, could alert her cellular phone to beep and remind her to pick up some milk as she passed the store on the way home from work.

As computers flow into our environments — whether they shrink into voice-operated eyeglasses or become merely a conference speaker and a portable screen— our ambience will be invested with more and more consciousness and, eventually, more autonomy. The delegation of intelligence to appliances and machines in our environment means that we are building an intermediary layer of consciousness around us: as interfaces become more intimate, this externalized intelligence, like a proto-intelligent cocoon that we are weaving about us, will become a cognitive extension of our own minds.

HIDDEN ROBOTS

When we think of robots, at least robots as they exist now, we tend to think of car-assembly robots, or the R2D2 type of units that work in a handful of hospitals, carrying medications and instruments from floor to floor. The only domestic robot currently retailed is the Black & Decker solar-powered lawnmower, which wanders around lawns by itself, cutting grass on sunny days.

These examples are mobile, autonomous units, easily identifiable as robots in the conventional sense. But, if we remove "mobility" from our definition of what makes a robot a robot, then, in a certain sense, robots already surround us. They are being implanted into our technological environment as "smart" functions in service electronics. It is as if we haven't learned to recognize such robots because they look nothing like we expected them to. These "static robots" scan channels for us in our car radios; they search CDs for individual songs. Static robots operate and man our telephone switches; they aim the antennae on our satellite dishes; and increasingly they oversee the operation of our cars and airplanes.

Robots are gestating inside our machines. They haven't yet birthed themselves from their electromechanical wombs. Perhaps they will never need to. It may be that the artificial entities that we will have to reckon with one day will not inhabit the faltering, mobile units that now represent state-of-the-art robotics. They may, rather, emerge abruptly from immobile data banks as artificial entities spawned by sheer complexity.

DOMESTIC ROBOTS

One of the few developments that seem to be overlooked by current futurists (with the exception of Hans Moravec) is the inevitable rise of domestic robots. Affordable domestic robots, linked to both home computers and cellular telephones, should (according to Moravec) be available to middle-class families within twenty to twenty-five years.

The ubiquity of domestic robots will present some interesting dilemmas. Domestic robots will have to be equipped with remote-control overrides, not only for convenience, but also for safety. Imagine that you own a mobile domestic aid. It is linked with your smart house, but it also has a degree of autonomy. You're renovating your house and decide to leave for a vacation with your family during the worst part of the construction. Halfway to the cottage, you remember that you left the stove on. Normally the smart house would turn off the stove, but the renovations have temporarily left the stove disconnected from your system. Unsure as to whether or not your robot can handle this situation by itself (even though the salesperson at the showroom assured you that many unforeseen situations unique to your house, family and pets could be learned by your robot), you decide to override it and use it as a remote proxy. You dial your robot and key in the override code that allows you to look through its "eyes" as you joystick through the house, towards the stove. Suddenly, everything stops. You press the joystick forward, but still no movement. Then, in an articulate, synthetic voice, the robot reminds you that the contractors have opened a hole in the floor. Your path would have taken the robot into it. You realize, with some chagrin, that you'd forgotten about that hole. Your robot wouldn't let you continue, even though it was contravening your commands, because robots are expensive and, ultimately, it was in your best interest to save it from damaging itself.

This hypothetical scenario might well be the beginning of a contest that will eventually be "won" by robots (though we will have to be patient). Small-scale skirmishes are already starting, for instance, the smart copying machines that annoyingly shut themselves off until you follow their self-servicing instructions, even if you know better and are trying to override that feature to do a job that doesn't fit the copier's normal programs. These struggles are the beginning of a push-and-shove relationship between humans and intelligent machines, and it is in these frustrating encounters with stubborn and limited machine intelligences that we see the beginning of a sibling rivalry, itself the prologue for a symbiosis that will bootstrap both machine intelligence and humans into the posthuman age. This is the reason why we don't have to worry about robots waging war on humans at some future armageddon. Hostilities have already broken out.

And yet human beings are extraordinarily adaptive creatures. The first generation of children to grow up with domestic robots will relate emotionally to their robotic peers. Inevitably, somewhere, sometime, truant parents, unable to find a baby-sitter, will post a robot in the nursery, its eyes trained on their sleeping son or daughter. If the child wakes up and begins to cry, a signal will automatically be sent to the infant's mother. Using telepresence, she might have the robot dangle a toy in front of the child, or perhaps even pick up her child and rock it. In this manner, intermittently at first, infants will learn from their first moments in the world to imprint on and trust robots. Later, as toddlers, competing with domestic robots, they might even play tricks on the robots, draping towels over their eyes so they can't see, then tripping them. This play will require the design of special software that will allow domestic robots to deal with active and mischievous physical competitors. Eventually this process will have an evolutionary influence on domestic robots. It will act like fast-forward natural selection, and enhance their mobility and intelligence. Quite literally, they will "grow up" and develop along with human children in an accelerated evolutionary process.

Chapter 8

ARTIFICIAL INTELLIGENCE

DEEP BLUE

In February 1996, and then again in May 1997, the world's best chess player competed against a computer. The matches were between an IBM supercomputer nicknamed "Deep Blue" and Garry Kasparov, the reigning world chess champion. The first match ended in one win for Deep Blue, three wins for Kasparov, and two draws. Some of the games lasted six hours. Garry Kasparov won the first match, but towards the end of that series his adviser said, "Garry is more exhausted than I've ever seen him." Kasparov, after studying Deep Blue's weaknesses, agreed to the rematch in 1997. However, IBM programmers had also fine-tuned Deep Blue's RS/6000 parallel processing software. The rematch was disastrous for Kasparov, ending in two wins for the computer, two wins for Kasparov and two draws. The posthuman era had dawned.

Chess was one area of human expertise thought safely beyond machine capabilities. That is no longer the case. Although computers like Deep Blue rely on brute speed and processing volumes, their programs will soon be modified to include pattern recognition. Strategy, foresight and psychology, hitherto believed to be intrinsically human attributes, can be duplicated, and even exceeded, by a computer program. The 1997 Deep Blue match was possibly the last time a human would ever win against a computer.

Sceptics can say that the games won by Deep Blue were actually won by the half-dozen IBM programmers who worked on the software, that the computer contains no innate intelligence or chess ability but is merely the sum of its instructions. This logic is compelling at first, until you consider that were the same group of programmers to play collectively against Kasparov, they would lose. When the program plays chess, it *exceeds* the programmers' collective abilities, proving that a computer can be designed to exceed the abilities of its designers. Certainly Kasparov took Deep Blue's abilities seriously when he called their first match "species-defining."

Also, to say that the computer or the program didn't win the match because it wasn't thinking for itself is to fall into the trap of presuming that there is something magical about human thought that allows us to think for ourselves, as if there were a little despot somewhere in our heads who runs our neurons and synapses. Since we don't think for ourselves any more than a computer does, how cognition gets done is irrelevant if the end result is identical.

We could be complacent about losing primacy in this singular area of human competence if it weren't that computers are quickly gaining in other areas as well. When Doug Lenat's CYC project (entering common sense and general knowledge into computers) is completed in several years, computers will graduate out of the idiot-savant stage. Eventually, all subroutines of our highest attributes will be duplicated, and perhaps exceeded, by computers. The final fusion of these diverse skills will be artificial intelligence. We might then console ourselves with the notion that, in art at least, machines (who are, after all, unemotional and unfeeling) will not be able to rival us. But this is falling into the trap of anthropomorphizing the basis of our own consciousness, our complex primate brain. If artificial intelligence resembles our consciousness, it will, at the very least, possess a rudimentary emotional repertoire as part of its self-governing reward-and-punishment circuits. The emotional foundation for true art will be laid alongside them.

THE CHARACTER OF ARTIFICIAL INTELLIGENCE

Hugo de Garis, a computer scientist working for ATR laboratories in Japan, is co-ordinating the creation of an ambitious computer. The computer is being called a "silicon brain" and, when it is completed in the year 2001, it will have more than a billion artificial neurons. What is extraordinary about this brain is the fact that it is designing itself. Its neurons are "cellular automata," every one of which has its own computer program. Each automaton grows its own linkages with the other cellular automata; once interconnected in a neural network, the automata will form a massively parallel computer. De Garis calls this form of self-directed, internally constructed neural network a "Darwin Machine" because the computer is using evolutionary engineering to design itself.

Strategies

Hugo de Garis's project is just one example of dozens of research programs in laboratories throughout the world that are racing towards artificial intelligence. There are two central strategies for attaining artificial intelligence: the first consists of making such a detailed likeness of the human brain that the property of consciousness is achieved; the second enlists artificial biology — self-guiding "evolutionary programs" which might eventually produce sentient intelligences.

If artificial intelligence is moulded in the likeness of its creators (as the former strategy would have it), the first artificial intelligence will be imprinted, behaviourally and emotionally, with the character of its human/scientific birth. Sheer joy of cognition and fierce curiosity about the world around it will be its prime motivations. The first artificial intelligence may well be science made conscious. If the second technique, synthetic evolution, produces the first artificial intelligence (even though it will exist only virtually at first), then this entity may turn out to be profoundly alien to our mode of consciousness, for it will have had a completely independent evolution.

SINGULARITY

Shortly after the creation of the first computer, ENIAC, over fifty years ago, the mathematician John von Neumann used the term "singularity" to describe the point at which humans will create an artificial super-intelligence. It was during a conversation at a mathematics conference that, as he later recalled, he first articulated idea that "the ever accelerating progress of technology and changes in the mode of human life ... give the appearance of approaching some essential singularity in the history of the race beyond which, human affairs, as we know them, could not continue."

Optimistic computer scientists predict that the singularity will occur within four decades in any of several ways. The most obvious and direct route will be the symbiotic union of humans and computers. With neural implants (a concept so overused in science fiction that it already seems outdated), the performance of the human mind could be boosted well beyond current capabilities. On the other hand, we might create, *fait accompli*, a single supercomputer that becomes spontaneously conscious, a new and sophisticated life form. Possibly, we will link computing networks into a supercomputer that spawns emergent consciousness. Finally, biotechnology might enhance the cellular structure of our brains to boost our own organic intelligence.

Mind Children

Whatever its genesis, superhumanity is probably inevitable (barring catastrophe). The advent of the posthuman era will be poignant because humans, as we currently know ourselves, will be superseded and will pass from centre stage. As one scientist replied when asked whether he was worried that intelligent machines might one day replace humans, "I'll throw my chips in on the side of intelligence, whatever form it may take." But this process will not be abrupt, and we will not be pushed aside like assembly-line workers being replaced by robots. It would be foolish to think we would design machines to supplant us, something humans would never do. We *will*, however, design machines that will bootstrap our species into the next, self-guided evolutionary stage. This will be an incremental and wholly voluntary processs. It is in our best interests to accept our intellectual progeny, our "mind children," as Hans Moravec calls the future generations of artificially intelligent beings, because they are a natural extension of our own evolution.

Literary Precedents

In Lord Dunsany's 1951 novel, *The Last Revolution* (published one year after Alan Turing predicted that we would have thinking machines by the end of the century), the protagonist is a scientist who succeeds in constructing an intelligent robot. What makes this book utterly convincing is Dunsany's description of the protagonist's girlfriend first encountering his artificially intelligent robot, which resembles a mechanical crab (it has four segmented, jointed legs and compound eyes like an insect). Instantly she knows, just looking at it, that it is "alive," a conscious entity. She is terrified. This instinctual reaction to another kind of consciousness might well be a romanticization, but there could also be some truth to it. Later in Dunsany's novel, the protagonist's dog attacks the artificial entity because "it has no smell." The dog also recognizes a living being, but one so alien that the dog is frightened. In self-defence the entity rips the dog to pieces. Although Dunsany's book over-dramatizes the alien qualities of an artificial entity, it does reveal our underlying anxiety about the new world we are creating.

Approaching the Singularity

Vernor Vinge, a science fiction writer and mathematician at San Diego State University, writes, "Another symptom of progress towards the Singularity: ideas themselves should spread even faster and even the most radical will quickly become commonplace. When I began writing science fiction in the middle '60s, it seemed very easy to find ideas that took decades to percolate into the cultural consciousness; now the lead time seems more like eighteen months."

In the sixties, the mathematician I.J. Good wrote, "an ultraintelligent machine could design even better machines; there would unquestionably be an 'intelligence explosion'; and the intelligence of man would be left far behind. Thus the first ultraintelligent machine is the last invention that man need ever make." But we must ask ourselves: if we are able to achieve immortality and inconceivable intelligence, what would be our relation (as posthumans) to our original selves? Would self, as we currently know it, become an empty sign? Ego, as neuroscientists would have it, is simply an illusion anyway. But what happens when your self can be copied or duplicated? Or what happens if parts of your "self" can be merged with other beings or supercomputers? What happens to language when you can communicate directly without words, by neurotelepathy facilitated by technology? What will become of our sense of self when, with genetic engineering, we can change our bodies into almost any shape? Also, if the posthuman sensibility is finer and more sophisticated than our own, would today's finest artistic creations seem, to our successors, like the incoherent grunting of baboons? And if the new consciousness grows out of the old, what of those who are left behind? What of those who, for religious, personal or socio-economic reasons, do not join the exodus? What will become of them?

SACRIFICIAL INTELLIGENCE

A large proportion of American artificial-intelligence research is funded by the military. Tragically, the first primitive, but possibly sentient, artificial intelligence we create might well be a slave consciousness, the brain of a tactical weapon. Furthermore, this sentience might exist for only a few seconds, just enough time to realize the last term of Descartes's *Cogito*, "I am," before it reaches its target — a kamikaze consciousness destined for annihilation a few seconds after it achieves awareness.

If our first use of silicon entities is born out of a heartless exploitation of their capabilities, it will be no wonder if those entities, if they have any autonomy at all, ultimately reject their makers. We may well reap our own inheritance. Our artificial descendants will be justly sceptical of humans, with our seemingly limitless capacity for violence and cruelty.

Chapter 9

CYBERMORPHS AND AVATARS: Simulations, Virtual Reality and Telepresence

TRANSMIGRATION IN VIDEO GAMES AND SIMULATIONS

Proprioception

There is a sixth sense in addition to the standard five. It is called "proprioception" and is our sense of bodily position, the "outline" of our form. Because it can effortlessly extend out of the body into whatever tool or vehicle we control, proprioception is one of our most abstract, and therefore most easily discorporealized, senses. For example, when you hold a pencil with your eyes closed, you can "feel," and in most cases guess, the identity of various surfaces that you drag the tip of the pencil against. The textures of glass, sand and paper can all be easily identified. You also use extensile proprioception when you drive a car. It allows you to make judgments, often to within a two-inch tolerance, of where the front bumper is, even though you cannot see it — your proprioception has flowed into the outline of the car. This phenomenon is referred to as having the "feel" of the car.

Video Games, Cybermorphs and Avatars

We use another form of proprioception in video games. Video games are like monoscopic virtual realities that we inhabit with manipulatable cybermorphs (the figures we use to represent ourselves in cyberspace). Our degree of identification with a cybermorph, using a sort of displaced proprioceptive projection into the virtual space, is almost total. When his cybermorph flies or falls, the sensation of flying and falling is very real for the game player. This is identification beyond mere projection; the game player *is* the cybermorph. It does not matter if the screen is small, large or three-dimensional. Scale is as completely mutable as proprioceptive consciousness is transferable. Two players connected to the same game, with individual screens, as when children play double Nintendo a couple of feet away from each other, are actually experiencing a shared virtual space.

In the virtual media, the displaced proprioceptive body becomes a site for bodily transformations. In certain video games, such as Killer Instinct, the cybermorph controlled by the game player has physical properties never before experienced by humans in the real world. Killer Instinct cybermorphs have the capability to morph their bodies; they can throw fire and melt into puddles.

With video games and virtual worlds, we are conditioning ourselves to somatic transformations. This concept is not new for us; we have, through the ages, imagined all sorts of fantastic incarnations for ourselves, from Proteus to transformers (the action-figure robot toys with interlocking moving parts that form different figures). The only difference is that we can now "be" our chimeras in our virtual spaces. This ability satisfies an innate property of human consciousness: the mutable, ever-changing and restless shape-shifter that lies at the core of our abstract human intelligence.

Rebirth and Transmigration

One of my favourite computer simulation-games is SIM ANT, by Maxis. In SIM ANT, a player controls a single ant. If that ant is attacked or threatened, the player can transfer into any other ant he designates. The area of the simulation includes a house and backyard, and the surface-to-simulation ratio is a surprising (compared with all other simulations) 80 percent at maximum magnification. In the yard are predatory spiders, ant lions, caterpillars, and an enemy nest of red ants who are your black ants' competition for food. Your ants lay pheromone trails (observed with a special screen setting), build tunnels and combat sporadic raids by the red ants.

Maxis also markets the very popular simulation/game SIM CITY, among others, but, for me, SIM ANT is the most successful of the simulations because it is at the right scale to represent a portion of insect reality so accurately that it doesn't suffer in comparisons with reality. In this way SIM ANT is much more realistic than SIM CITY. Even though some writers have claimed to have had the sensation that foreign cities they visited were scaled-up versions of the simulations in SIM CITY, that feeling has never struck me. However, playing SIM

ANT I have had the border between simulation and reality blur. One summer, after a particularly intense session of SIM ANT, I walked outside and saw an ant on the sidewalk. I had the eerie feeling that, if I had my trackball and pointer, I could operate the ant. Furthermore, I knew the ant was in "forage mode" and I could almost guess what the approximate population of its home nest was.

The key point about this particular simulation is that, if your ant is killed by another ant, or a spider, or by being stepped on by a human, it, or I should say you, are reborn (after undergoing a fast-forward metamorphosis from egg to grub to pupa to adult). In essence, the soul of the white ant is resurrected, just as the controllable figure in video games is reborn when a player starts a new game. Rebirth and trans-migration, first graphically introduced in cartoons, are basic assumptions in video games and computer simulations.

PROPRIOCEPTION AND TELEPRESENCE

Our proprioceptive capability extends into most media. It is second nature for us to be in two places at once while we are on the telephone, or to identify so completely with a video-game cybermorph that we jerk involuntarily when our cyber-morph runs into something. With telepresence, however, propriocepton is taken to a new level.

Telepresence, as the name suggests, is the ability to see and manipulate remote objects using a robot proxy. Currently, robot proxies are limited to a handful of applications, usually in hostile environments, such as deep-ocean salvage and the remotely piloted police robots that are used to disarm bombs.

The 1997 Mars probe used a robot proxy (with, interestingly enough, a limited amount of autonomy) called *Sojourner*.

In current leading-edge telepresence research laboratories (the Human Machine Interaction Laboratory at Carnegie Mellon University, for instance), remote piloting is taken much further. "Teleoperators" wear a harness that incorporates skin-pressure sensors, and a headpiece with two tiny video screens, one for each eye, that provide stereoscopic vision. Two speakers transmit stereo sound from the remote location. If the robot proxy is equipped with "arms" and "hands," the pressure solenoids in the gloves can also transmit tactile texture.

The harness, connected to the robot proxy, transmits the teleoperator's actions to the proxy. When she reaches out to touch something, the arm on the robot proxy reaches out at exactly the same time. When she hears a noise and looks for its source in the remote location, the robot proxy's camera and microphone array turns and focuses on the sound's point of origin at the same time as she does. She is literally having an out-of-body experience. The incoming signals can be amplified or modified in a number of ways. The visual signal can be modified to provide night vision, or even infrared vision. The proxy robot's "hearing" can also be amplified to give the teleoperator hypersonic hearing in the remote location.

So much for real-world interactions. The harness can also transmit signals to and from a *virtual* robot proxy that exists as a simulation in a computer. The experience for the teleoperator is identical in every way to the experience of operating an actual robot proxy in the field.

The potential for recreational use of robot proxies will soon be too profitable to ignore. Proxy robots will be able to fight to the "death" in front of paying audiences; they will be capable of battling each other in survival games without injury to either of their teleoperators. Plans to merchandise robot proxy moon-walks have already been registered. The experience of telepresence, whether in virtual environments with VR glasses and joysticks, or via sophisticated robot proxies, should eventually become commonplace and affordable. Most people not only will be comfortable with the amplified and extraordinary existences of robot proxies, but will become habituated to them. Our dependency on the strength and power of our proxies might, in fact, become so great that we will be unwilling to return to our relatively weak bodies. When we have the potential to connect our nervous systems directly into a proxy humanoid, our eventual exodus from our biological bodies may seem more inviting.

If Moravec's prediction that human consciousness will be transferable to an artificial platform actually transpires, then uploading consciousness directly into the proxy humanoid is a logical extension. This could well be a smooth transition point for the metamorphosis from the transhuman to a posthuman era. It is more likely, however, that the process of transition will be so piecemeal, and will take place over so long period of time, that the point of demarcation between transhuman and posthuman may not be clear to those undergoing it.

Importantly, both recreational and applied telepresence could have another, totally unanticipated effect. Telepresence might become the first medium in which we will become conceptually adept at out-of-body experiences. The process has already begun. Two years ago, a telepresence researcher (John Merritt, at a facility in Williamsburg, Massachussetts) was operating a mobile proxy robot in another room in the building he was in. He decided to pilot the mobile unit from its testing room through the building and into the room in which his operating terminal was located. He identified with the robot proxy so completely that, when the proxy came into the room in which he was actually sitting, he saw himself as a total stranger. He said the experience was eerily unnerving, claiming it was similar to an experience we've probably all had, where we catch a glimpse of ourselves in a store mirror before we recognize ourselves. The only difference, he said, was that, in this case, he couldn't shake the feeling of unfamiliarity after he'd identified himself.

As recreational applications of telepresence and virtual reality become more common, many of us are likely to become habituated to discarnate experiences. We will be used to having our "ghosted" identities nested within multidimensional, hallucinatory, virtual realities that will compose our own complex, everday realities. This blurring of somatic boundaries will prepare us for the very real, physical changes that biotechnology and various artificial implants will effect upon our bodies.

WALKMAN PERSONAL STEREOS AND VIRTUAL REALITY

Most people take Walkmans for granted. There is nothing new about mobile stereophonic sound. But personal sound systems have done more than take "living room" sound outdoors; they have established the social acceptability of wearing headphones, a type of perceptual prosthesis, in public. Furthermore, stereo music, particularly over headphones, is an aural, three-dimensional, virtual reality. Because sound doesn't interfere with vision, Walkmans can layer the music over out-side sound. The depth of this prosthetic overlay turns many Walkman users into virtual deaf/mutes who underestimate the volume of personal sounds. How many times have we heard the tuneless humming of Walkman users or their inappropri-ately loud public flatulence? Nevertheless, we routinely accept humans who are partially immersed in an artificial perceptual environment as socially invisible and unremarkable. Portable sound systems (as well as cellular phones) are just the beach-head of a whole series of layered, electronic environments that will soon be complicating our perceptual reality.

VIRTUAL REALITY

Cyber-sickness: The Future on Hold

Cyber-sickness, the dizzy spells and flashbacks that plague airline pilots after training sessions in virtual-reality flight simulators, also affects anyone wearing virtual reality goggles, particularly those systems with body-motion sensors. So it is that fears of massive lawsuits have delayed the introduction of mainstream virtual reality, Nintendo being the only company to release a commercial virtual-reality game system, Virtual Boy, and even it has been constrained; its VR glasses are not wearable, but are mounted on a tripod in order to prevent cyber-sickness. Sega, on the other hand, seems to be waiting for the cyber-sickness wrinkle to be ironed out. The slump of interest in virtual reality systems has pushed companies such as Virtuality Ltd. (a manufacturer of arcade-sized VR mod-ules) into receivership.

The potential for virtual reality, if cyber-sickness can be cured, is unlimited. It will allow us to enter worlds of our own creation, on any scale we choose. Educational and museum displays will be upgraded from two-button video stations to VR simulations that enable us to walk through Cretaceous forests and watch grazing dinosaurs, wander into Egyptian pyramids or walk along the bottom of the deepest oceans. We will hover in space among the stars, and pilot ourselves along the major arteries of the human body. But it all must wait for a solution to the dilemma of cyber-sickness.

Virtual-Reality Interfaces

Virtual-reality completely melts the interface between human and computer, because the computer program *becomes* the physical environment. It is as if, upon discovering computers, we have finally found an intelligent species that we can teach not only to speak our language, but also to help us construct our *next* language.

Perhaps present-day notions of virtual reality, where body sensors relay data about our movements into the computer that is running our virtual reality, will disappear with the advent of "internalized" virtual reality. Internalized simulations mediated by neural implants would run entirely in our heads, without our bodies having to enact our movements within virtual reality. We will not be sleepwalkers acting out our dream, but, rather, lucid dreamers. However, until that point is reached, holographically-based virtual realities will probably be the next goal of virtual reality.

Chapter 10

WORLD SELF: Telecommunications and the Art of Transhumanism

THE DISTORTION OF SPACE BY THE MEDIA

Media disorient us; telephones, for example, allow us to be in two places at once, and films give us impossible vantages on the world — aerial panoramas, fibre-optic views of internal organs, and so on. At the same time as the physical world is being downloaded into the media as content, our experience of the physical world is being distorted by the media. The media have skewed our personal perception of space and time as well. None of these effects is particularly obvious to us however, because our sense of dislocation is submerged beneath the utility and thrall of our media.

Not only do our media dislocate us, but our senses have begun to overlap as the media condition us to perceive things in terms of alternative sensory modalities — television as tactile, radio as visual. Synesthesia, the apprehension of one sense for another, such as seeing sounds or smelling colours, has become a side effect of electronic media as they metaphorize the world. The media constantly depict inter-sensory translations; for example, colours and images often represent music in rock videos and cartoons.

Additionally, we spend an increasing amount of time immersed in artificial realities created by the media; on the tele-phone, at our computers, or watching television. Consequently, these realities have become commonplace. Our familiarity with discarnate perception and sensory teleportation means that we are beginning to accept ourselves as discorporate, free-floating consciousnesses — entities that are habituated to moving at the speed of light, to being in two places at once (telephones and teleconferencing), and to having our physical shapes altered, at least proprioceptively, in video games and virtual realities. By extending our senses beyond our bodies through the electronic media, we have initiated a migration out of our bodies.

THE INTERNET

Epistolary Renaissance

Although the Internet is a relatively new utility, it will soon be as commonplace as telephones, cable TV and running water. Right now the Internet is in a transitional phase, and conse-quently many of the operating skills required during this period are provisional and will become redundant as soon as better software and faster graphic interfaces are available. The eventual compatibility of telephone and Internet services will reduce our current reliance on keyboard interfaces, with the result that the Net will undergo another demographic surge. Voice recognition will obviate the need for keyboards permanently.

Until keyboards are transcended by new technologies, the popularity of the Net will continue to produce a vast epistolary flowering such as the world hasn't seen since the Victorian era. At present, the Internet is a huge e-mail pen-pal network that relies on literacy to function. As a result, literacy skills are undergoing a minor renaissance. This current period of transition in the Internet parallels that in film technology in the mid-1920s. Speech in films was limited to subtitles until the development of sound technology in the late 1920s. It is unlikely, though, that we will wait a decade for voice capability in the Internet. Within a few years, laborious keyboard communications will seem as quaint as the command codes that were necessary to run early IBM PCs, and with their disappearance our temporary epistolary flowering will also fade away.

What might take longer is the arrival of the real "Information Age," via the World Wide Web. Certainly, the Web is both informative and engaging, particularly for collective experiences like the Mars Sojourner exploration, as well as some exceptional individual and institutional sites, but it's hardly the "infobahn" we've been promised. The full potential of the Web will only be achieved after a monumental, global labour, more intensive than the Human Genome Project, wherein all public domain books in the major libraries of the world are methodically scanned and downloaded into virtual libraries. This immense task should be started immediately. Until the entirety of human knowledge is available to anyone with access to the Web, we are just kidding ourselves about an information revolution.

Posthuman Receptacle

Perhaps there is another, collective, yet subconscious, impulse for the lemming-like scramble to get on the Net. Perhaps we intuitively know that the Internet is the necessary forerunner of the collective mind. And perhaps we also know that, in the posthuman realm, we will need a complex, spacious and fully virtualized world to satisfy the innate human need for three-dimensional mobility (even if it is "virtual") if the physical body is to be left behind.

THE GLOBAL POSITIONING SYSTEM

The Global Positioning System (GPS) is a worldwide electronic navigation system deployed for American military use but recently made available to civilians with special receivers. Ocean-going fishermen have been using the GPS for years. It enables them to fish in exactly the same place, day after day, even when they are out of sight of land and unable to locate any landmarks. With a GPS receiver, anyone, anywhere on Earth, can pick up a satellite signal that will give her exact position to within several yards.

A satellite-broadcast navigation system, such as the GPS, is a technological abstraction of the notion of place. It negates landscape by blinding us, turning travel into a game of "hot or cold." The GPS is a practical abstraction that enables travellers to operate on the surface of the planet independently of terrain, features and locales. This free-floating, rootless, auto-pilot sensibility turns us into a nomadic people, perpetually ready to abandon the substance of our world. To bypass terrain is to banish true exploration.

The GPS is another link in the electronic web around our planet and, consequently, around nature. The surface of our planet has been translated into the silicon architecture of a telecommunications/data network that can plot the movement of any individual with a receiver. We are now encased in a virtual grid within an electric, Cartesian cocoon.

Because the GPS means we can never be lost, the state of being lost may become not only an anachronism, but an almost privileged state of intoxication. The GPS is the digital shepherd, to whom we can relinquish control and become passengers. It makes us tourists with a perfect, artificial sense of direction.

GRASPING THE WORLD

The Memory Theatre

In *The Art of Memory*, Francis Yates describes Giulio Camillo's wooden "memory theatre," a structure that Camillo built in Italy during the years 1530 to 1532. This structure was the reverse of a normal theatre; it was built for a single person only, and that person occupied its "stage." When Camillo stood upon his stage and looked out at his "audience," he saw instead seven horizontal tiers consisting of hundreds of carved, wooden drawers. In these drawers, unseen, were the collected works of the Roman orator Cicero, which Giulio had memorized, using his theatre as an aid.

Camillo's memory theatre functioned as a mnemonic device for apprehending the entirety of Cicero's work (an encyclopedic collection) at once. In a sense, Camillo's memory theatre was a predecessor of the encyclopedia, because it led immediately to Giordano Bruno's memory theatre several decades later. Giordano Bruno, a medieval scholar, magician and alchemist, took Camillo's system and enlisted it in his attempt to compile all human knowledge up to that point in one mnemonic system.

Today the size and complexity of human knowledge make it too vast to condense into a supercomputer, no less a mnemonic system. Yet, we all strive, in some way, to grasp the ungraspable, to contain the world and its complexity in one cathartic experience. Our worldwide telecommunications net is adding another layer of complexity, but it is also embedding/implanting connectivity into the world, like the sentient rhizomes of some vast, interconnected intelligence. Thus, more complexity might help us achieve true omniscience, when coupled with artificially enhanced human intelligence.

Perpetual Upgrading as an End in Itself

There are many occasions in our lives when, if we are in a hurry, we must operate a system despite our having incomplete knowledge of it, for instance, when we learn new technologies — a new word-processing system or an unfamiliar appliance. Just before we master a new system, there is a stage of false confusion that we experience, an interval of competence without confidence, when we are still not sure we "get it." (This interval is a microcosmic version of the overarching feeling we have when trying to comprehend the world's complexity. We know the direction of a solution, we know "where" the world is, but we can comprehend it only in its parts, not in its entirety. Our innate urge to experience the world's totality is at the heart of mystical yearning, and the world is a metaphor for an omniscient knowledge that may forever elude us.)

In one sense, a provisional worldview in progress is more useful than one that is systematized, because the world itself is ongoing and continually in process. It is only when we are learning that we mirror the continuous transformation of the world. The perpetual upgrading of software systems and computer technologies gives us a metaphor of a "work in progress" that is a useful microcosm of our aspiration to total knowledge. This aspiration may be more desirable than the end product, or world knowledge, because our understanding of the world/universe must necessarily be incomplete. In other words, an intimation of world knowledge gives us a "fix" on complete knowledge, satisfying the desire for the end without sacrificing the means.

THE RANDOM

Coincidence is four-dimensional, situated in both time and space. The variegated flow of phenomena, overlapping the paths of moving entities, produces random confrontations that can be significant for the participants: the awkward encounter with an ex-partner in an unlikely restaurant; the unfortunate conjunction of a gazelle and a hungry lion at the same watering hole. Accidental meetings throw together individuals who would normally, statistically speaking, be separated widely in space and time.

Evolution is driven by change, and change relies on chance. Random mutations give rise to useful modifications. The play of randomness is time-based and, over long periods, becomes statistically constant. Different species interacting also modify each other — statistically recurring coincidences and random encounters become, over time, engines of natural selection. For example, if many individual lions encounter gazelles often enough at waterholes, then lions, as a species, flourish. But at the individual, sub-statistical level, chance is experienced as dynamic and capricious, even wilful.

Our personal characterization of the random is strongest just after a significantly traumatic or powerful random event, such as winning a lottery or being in a car accident. The trauma of the random makes us vaguely paranoid, makes us feel, however briefly, that we "know" what is behind this force. Religious interpretations often arise. But to understand chance in its own terms, empirically, we have to refrain from characterizing it all. The random cannot be located or predicted. It can only be experienced intuitively in the thrall of its recent occurrence.

We humans are fascinated by chance because it is responsible for some of the most significant interventions in our lives. Gambling is a form of "surfing" chance, and we have devised many magical systems that purport to predict random events. Everything from the Tarot to bone oracles claims to have an inside track. The random is one of the essential elements of the world. It is a dominant motif of nature, and of the universe in general. Galaxies, pebbles, clouds, trees — all are randomly distributed. Even crystals have random relations to each other. The random is worthy of awe and reverence, though any predictive system of religion goes against its essential nature. Of all the world's religions and philosophies, only Taoism, Zen Buddhism and science seem to be capable of embracing its impartial machinations.

Even though it surrounds us at every moment and is somehow at the basis of existence, the random is still beyond our technical grasp. Random-number generators, useful in all sorts of mathematical and computational applications, are based on algorithmic models of randomness, and are only approximations of the random. Scientists and mathematicians still have to resort to natural sources for precise random-number generators. It may be that the purely random will turn out to be the natural phenomenon most resistant to synthetic duplication.

RADIO, TELEPHONES AND THE LOSS OF AMBIENCE

In one sense the content of radio is not the program; rather, the ambience of the atmosphere is. Radio waves consist of electromagnetic soundings of an invisible world of solar storms, electrical interference and distant radio signals reflected off layers in the atmosphere.

Like the telephone, radio is an intimate, aural experience of the speed of light. Although both telephone and radio signals travel at the speed of light, they are distinct because of the nature of their conducting medium. The non-cellular telephone signal travels inside a cable as a series of contained and unidirectional pulses of current. By contrast, a radio signal is uncontained. Radio signals are spherically expanding electromagnetic wave fronts that are susceptible to the electromagnetic ecologies of the Earth and Sun.

The advent of cellular phones is changing the cable telephone signal into a radio signal, particularly in this transitional period when cellular technology is still in its early stages. Artifacts of radio transmission are insinuating themselves into our telephone conversations — intermittent loss of signal, overlapping or faint signals and static, all originating from the atmospheric medium of radio. At the same time, radio, through the increasing use of cable delivery, is converging on telephone technology, removing the normal ambient qualities of the radio signal.

This convergence of transmission media will become more typical in the next few decades, as channels once used exclusively for a single medium are used for two or more others. Eventually, fully digital signals, containing voice, video or music, will choose whatever path is convenient and cheapest at the time of transmission. This means that the ambient, coincidental artifacts of the various media — artifacts that gave those media their sensual characteristics — will no longer be identifiable. They will be blended into a meta-medium, rarely unpredictable in its background characteristics, and dependable for signal transmission.

HUMANS AS COMMUNICATORS

Nothing beats a live human being for conveying information. That's why the trend in schools to have TVs and computers replace teachers is worrisome. When we are attempting to learn something, or trying to acquire information of any sort, it is always more efficient to be taught by an expert person rather than by a film, book or manual. Humans have a wide communicative band width, communicating synopsized information on several levels at the same time. We gesture to demonstrate spatial metaphors, we have nuances of expression in voice tone, our eye movements and body postures all transmit subverbal data. The sophisticated, multichannelled, high-speed nature of human communication is always quicker and more efficient, and will be so for quite some time to come.

Chapter 11

BIOTECHNOLOGY

FIVE THOUSAND YEARS OF GENETIC ENGINEERING

Genetic engineering, in the form of eugenics, has been with us for thousands of years. Everything we eat, except fish, shellfish and a few other wild foods, is almost exclusively "genetically engineered," the product of hundreds, some- times thousands, of years of genetic manipulation by breeding. The corn we eat today bears little resemblance to its South American ancestor of two thousand years ago. We have transformed wild dogs into the monstrous shapes of dachshunds and chihuahuas; we have taken carp and turned them into bug-eyed goldfish with oversized fins; we've made feathers grow out of the feet of pigeons, and turned cows black and white. Genetic engineering is as basic to humans as language and tool-making. It has been stymied only by the time-based limitations of breeding (it takes hundreds of years to develop a new breed), but, with the advent of biotechnology, those limitations have been removed.

BIOTECHNOLOGY AND ENGINEERED EVOLUTION

> *It's morphing time.*
> — Mighty Morphin' Power Rangers

On May 22, 1989, W. French Anderson (chief of the molecular-hematology lab at the U.S. National Heart, Lung, and Blood Institute) got the approval of both the U.S. National Institutes of Health and the Food and Drug Administration to proceed with the first human gene therapy using retroviruses. This ruling paved the way for the first stage in the genetic transformation, or "morphing," of the human species. Gene therapy, the transduction of genes into human cells, allows doctors to change the genetic structure of humans in order to fight disease. With retroviral gene transduction and recombinant genetics — where genes are "operated" on and put together in new orders — two tools are in place that will be necessary for the next stage of self-guided evolution. The 1989 ruling is the beginning of our abandonment of natural evolution. From now on it we are doing it "our way."

Bioethics

Anderson suggested provisional ethical guidelines for gene therapy. He divided gene therapy, and its potential use, into four fields: *somatic gene therapy*, where normal genes are introduced into persons with defective genes; *germ-line gene therapy*, where corrective genes are introduced into the reproductive cells of a patient in order to prevent a specific disorder from being passed on to his or her children; *enhancement genetic engineering*, where the introduced genes correct a deficiency induced by hormones; and *eugenic genetic engineering*, where selected traits, such as intelligence or strength, are improved by gene therapy. These last two categories can also be achieved by recombinant genetics through direct manipulation of human germ cells.

The only field of gene therapy that Anderson has prohibited, via the FDA, is eugenic genetic engineering. His proscription cannot be enforced internationally, however, particularly because of its huge potential for profit. Eventually other bioengineers will fill the vacuum left by the U.S. ruling. When recombinant genetics and gene transduction become available in the international biotechnology market, they will allow wealthy parents to alter the genes of their children to give them even more of an advantage: beautiful features, violet eyes, high intelligence, along with extraordinary physical strength and grace. But they may not stop there — more imaginative (some might say more diabolical) parents will select unusual and rare features, mixing racial characteristics freely, or even developing a eugenic "aesthetics" that transcends normal values of physical beauty. Extralong fingers and necks, ears that come to points without lobes, and elaborate or enlarged genitals are all probable options.

Morphing Time

But the features that parents select for their children using genetic engineering will be conservative, I suspect, compared with the changes that individuals will wreak upon themselves. Cosmetic retroviral genetic engineering, at first the enclave of the very wealthy, might well become the testing ground of the first major genetic transformation of the human species.

When (and if) this happens, when biotechnology allows the rich to buy unearthly beauty, intelligence and functional immortality, an inevitable biological gap will open between upper-income earners and the biotechnological underclass. Imagine being temporarily unemployed and feeling a little disreputable in a future where the difference between wealth and poverty has created two species of humans. During a walk downtown one evening, you pause to stand outside a theatre to look at a crowd of well-dressed people milling at the entrance. A sleek black vehicle pulls up, and out of it steps a tall, angular woman. But this woman is not only as beautiful as any fashion model of today — she completely outclasses them. Her genetically engineered skin is bioluminescent; it literally glows in the dark. Shimmering gold and amber ripples pulsate faintly, slipping in eddies and waves that run along her neck and arms. Briefly, she turns to look at you, and, when she does, the setting sun catches her eyes for an instant. Her irises are bright gold, and her pupils are elliptical, like a cat's. Over her right shoulder hovers something that looks like a large insect. It darts over to you and hangs motionless in front of your face, its wings humming. You realize it is a small mechanical dragonfly. It is scanning and recording your features for the woman's security files.

When genetic alterations become more affordable, there will be an unanticipated bonus: for the first time in our history, we will be freed from the accident of our births, freed from the tyranny of permanently fixed features. We will also be freed from uniformity, and from the involuntary constraints of race.

Indeed, racial traits will become optional — a single, unremarkable variable within a panoply of choice.

Fear of Cloning

When Scottish bioengineers succeeded in cloning an adult sheep in 1996, legislators around the world reacted by prohibiting human cloning. U.S. president Bill Clinton announced a ban on the use of federal funds for human-cloning research. Certainly any inherent dangers within any new biotechnology must be anticipated, but to cater to hysteria by banning any research is perhaps even more dangerous in the long run because it might compromise the continued furtherance of human development

In one sense, human beings have been dealing with clones for as long as we have been human, for clones are really just time-delayed identical twins (triplets, quadruplets, etc.). There is nothing alien or new about clones, nor do we have to make any elaborate repositionings of our ethics or psychology to accept human cloning, although this is not to say that governments should permit private-sector human cloning before all the necessary testing has been done. On the other hand, the economic advantages of cloning animals has already been established for animal husbandry, and once the benefits of human cloning are demonstrable, human cloning will become difficult to reasonably oppose.

Ultimately, however, advances in biotechnology are crucial to the self-guided evolution of the human species. These advances must be both well considered and embraced, for we must guard against the danger that unreasonable fears will delay valuable research in bioengineering.

THE ECONOMY OF BIOTECHNOLOGY

Aside from whatever moral issues bioengineering, private eugenics and hormone therapies raise, there is the practical reality of a burgeoning biotechnology market. This lucrative market currently includes such products as the sperm of Nobel laureates for artificial insemination, and genetically engineered growth hormones. (Growth hormones, which currently rank fortieth on the list of best-selling drugs worldwide, are generally purchased by the anxious parents of undersize children.) Offshore facilities such as Valiant Ventures in the Bahamas are already offering to provide facilities for human cloning. Factor in the international trade in human organs, as well as life-enhancing hormone therapies purchased by the wealthy, and you have the core of a largely unregulated global market in biotechnology, a market that will be the arena within which most future advances of genetic engineering will take place, determined strictly by market demand.

Hopefully, the international biotechnology market will remain unregulated and out of the control of today's large, agricultural bioengineering corporations. In North America some of these firms have established bio-monopolies — patenting seeds and engineering crops that manufacture their own pesticide. These and other dangerous initiatives are taking place within a "regulated" market in North America. Presumably the competition of a world market will ensure a *de facto* de-regulation of global bioengineering, particularly if genetic "patents" are successfully pirated.

CRYONICS

Cryonics is becoming big business. There are several American cryonics firms — Alcor, Cryocare and Cryo Span, among others — and they have dozens of patients suspended in liquid nitrogen, awaiting future medical treatment. These patients have paid amounts ranging from $25,000 to $120,000 to be suspended. In the last decade cryonics (not "cryogenics," which is a popular misnomer) has moved from the quack zone into a lucrative corporate enterprise.

Cryopreservation may eventually be on a par with life insurance and wills. It was K. Eric Drexler's book, *Engines of Creation,* that elevated cryonics into scientific feasibility. Progress in cryonics is quickening: human embryos are routinely frozen, and a mammalian heart has been frozen in liquid nitrogen and then revived. If it becomes demonstrable that a future technology could reverse freezing damage, the cryonics industry will reap enormous profits as baby boomers, the legion of denial, sign up *en masse.*

In *Engines of Creation,* Drexler describes how nanotechnology will revive cryonically frozen humans. Nanomachinery, the size of microbes, along with nanocomputers to co-ordinate their activity, will be injected into the larger arteries and veins of frozen patients in order to clear their circulatory systems of cryonic protectant. After these first nanomachines have done their work, they would be flushed out, and a second wave of nanomachines would be pumped into the circulatory system. These new nanomachines (literally trillions of them) would be specialized in removing protectant from the interior of individual cells, molecule by molecule, until each cell was ready for the cellular-repair nanomachines.

After the protectant-removing nanomachines have been flushed out, the third wave of nanomachines, specialized in cellular repair, would be pumped into the patient. These would be the most specialized of all the nanomachines, and would include nanocomputers, one at least per cell, to direct the molecular repairs of the cells, using the molecular architecture of healthy cells as a template. At this stage whatever diseased tissue caused the patient's death would be automatically repaired.

Drexler then goes on to describe the final stages of the reanimation of a cryonic patient, detailing how fresh blood would be cloned from the patient's own cells and transfused back into the now warm body. The heart would be restarted, and the patient would emerge into a state of anesthesia. Doctors would then do an examination of all vital systems, before withdrawing the pumping apparatus from the chest cavity. There would be no scar from the procedure because the final few nanomachines would be used to re-fuse the chest. The patient would then be ready for reawakening.

One factor that has prevented cryonics from developing sooner has been market resistance, fuelled in part by people's intuitive reaction against the notion of cryonic suspension. There is something very unnatural, almost macabre, about the concept of suspension. It's as if the hope for immortality that attends it is not just perverse, but also a pathological denial that cheapens death. As well, we have no innate psychological mechanisms to prepare us for indefinite life spans. We are designed to die, both physically and psychologically.

Many human beings share a strong intuition, though, that part of us survives death, and from that intuition have arisen whole belief systems concerning immortality and the soul.

Perhaps that intuition is based on some deep knowledge that consciousness is something very different from biology and species, that it has its own agenda which extends beyond the carbon-based home it has now. Arguably neither immortality nor the "soul" exists in the real world, but technology might just make it possible for us to secure the existence of both in the future.

TICKLING THE DRAGON'S TAIL: VIRTUAL LIFE AND ARTIFICIAL BIOLOGY

Artificial Evolution

During the final phase of the Manhattan Project, the construction of the first atomic bomb at Los Alamos, in New Mexico, the critical mass of the plutonium had to be measured precisely before the bomb could be tested. This was done by placing the plutonium bricks destined for the bomb in a horseshoe-shaped pile that verged on critical mass. The atomic scientists then ran a small additional amount of plutonium through the pile (very quickly) and — for less than a second — the pile was measurably critical. This process was named, aptly, "tickling the dragon's tail."

Like atomic fission, evolution is a powerful primal force that until now has been in nature's hands. All that, it would seem, is about to change. Not only are we taking over our genetic development, but we are also using computers to simulate the very fundamental mechanisms of evolution. These simulations go beyond pure research; applications have already been found. Artificial evolution was used, for example, to create several of the software modules within Windows 95.

A new scientific discipline has sprung up over the past few decades. Called "artificial biology," it uses simulations to study life. Its most important discovery is the ability to model and perpetuate evolution within a computer simulation. These artificial evolutions are every bit as active and creative as real evolution is in nature, the only difference being that these artificial evolutions can be directed into areas completely untried by nature. If we can "harness" this evolutionary force, then computers will be able to innovate in ways we can neither conceive nor predict. As artificial biology continues its search through alternative evolutions, it will one day discover highly sophisticated potential life forms, life forms whose cellular and anatomical biology will be utterly alien to us. Artificial evolution is truly a form of "tickling the dragon's tail." But if some of these artificial life forms turn out to become conscious entities, we will be tickling much more than the tail of evolution's dragon.

Artificial Life

Computer viruses satisfy two of the criteria that define life forms — they replicate, and they survive. There are now several thousand computer viruses in existence, and a hundred new viruses are catalogued by computer-virus hunters every month. (Even more extraordinary is the fact that researchers believe that two or three of these viruses evolved spontaneously, without human intervention.) Not one of the hundreds of viruses catalogued to this point has become extinct.

Computer viruses are just the beginning of a synthetic ecology. There are already artificial life forms in certain multiple-user environments on the Web. Some multiple-user sites, such as Alpha World, have become ecologies, where artificial virtual life forms called "bots" wander through the cyberscape, independently of the users who also inhabit the virtual space. These virtual life forms, regardless of whether they are created or arise spontaneously within computer networks, are the forerunners of a virtual biology that will begin to create its own ecology within the Internet.

Virtual pets have already become popularized. They were an instant success story when they were introduced in 1997 by the Bandai Corporation of Tokyo. (Bandai was also responsible for "The Mighty Morphin' Power Rangers.") Their pets "from cyberspace," called Tamagotchis, sold four million units in their first three weeks on the U.S. market. It seems that we are more than ready for virtual life, and the consumer market for virtual pets will help drive the evolution of increasingly sophisticated digital life forms.

NANOTECHNOLOGY AND ARTIFICIAL LIFE

Imploding Frontiers

There is an economic impetus behind the race towards increasing miniaturization. As Western economies stagnate, the efficiency of doing more with less becomes more attractive as a way of maintaining growth. The vast capital expenditures necessary to open up space as a colonization and manufacturing frontier are prohibitive. Perhaps it is not a coincidence that, as the macro-frontier of space collapses, limited to shuttle missions and unmanned probes, the inner frontier is expanding. From telephones to computers, miniaturized technology now affects all of us, every day.

As a result, here at the cusp of the millennium, we are balanced between two seemingly infinite realms of exploration — outer space and micro-space — and there is evidence that the scales have already tipped in favour of the latter. By "shrinking space" we enlarge the efficiency of existing physical space by packing more complexity into smaller areas. The World Wide Web on the Internet, for example, has become a frontier of colonization. This frontier of inner space is particularly striking in VRML (virtual reality modelling language) worlds on the net, such as MUDs (multiple-user dungeons), or Alpha World — the multiple-user virtual city. In Alpha World and virtual cities like it, you can build your own virtual house and walk out the front door to roam the virtual streets. Alpha World already has thousands of inhabitants and is expanding exponentially. In fact, as this book goes to print, the total surface area of all virtual worlds on the Web is already seven times as large as the Earth's surface.

The virtues of micro-space are its immediacy and cheapness. You don't need to burn a million dollars' worth of rocket fuel to get there. Outer space, accessible only by outrageous expenditures of fuel and money, is still characterized by industrial technology. Without a radical advance in propulsion systems, outer space may turn out to be useful only as a limitless industrial park and garbage dump — and space colonies don't look likely as a viable solution to overpopulation on Earth, at least in the short term. As the world becomes more crowded, the benefits of micro-technology will pay off in spades.

Micro-technology will cross a quantum divide when nanotechnology is developed. K. Eric Drexler, in *Engines of Creation*, writes about the first replicators: bacteria-sized machines that, once constructed, will reproduce themselves. The term "singularity" (which, as I mentioned earlier, futurists, nanotechnologists and others use to describe the construction of the first artificial intelligence) is also sometimes used to refer to the moment when the first functional replicator is constructed. This term will not seem so melodramatic once the revolutionary effects of nanotechnology are understood. Even though Drexler himself insists that these nanomachines, or "nanofactories" as he calls them, are not artificial life, the door will be opened to the creation of truly artificial life once nanotechnology is in place. Once machines smaller than cells have been created, there is no reason why they cannot be linked together into synthetic tissues, organs and bodies, at which point the difference between living tissue and living machinery may cease to be discernible.

In *Engines of Creation*, Drexler speculates about how the first assemblers might construct the first replicators. Because assemblers are so small, he points out, an assembler arm will be able to move millions of times a second. Specifically programmed assemblers will create the first replicator, a self-reproducing nanomachine that can make unlimited copies of itself, given the necessary raw materials. In addition, each replicator will have an on-board nanocomputer composed of roughly 100 million atoms, acting, like DNA does in our own cells, to orchestrate the actions of the assembler.

A replicator will be able to copy itself at a rate of about 100 million atoms a second. However, even at that rate, Drexler points out, it would take fifteen minutes to make a single copy of itself, and a century to make "a respectable speck." But that is not, Drexler goes on to explain, how replicators will operate. Drexler then describes how miraculous — and massive — the replication process will be. Drexler writes:

> Thus the first replicator assembles a copy in one thousand seconds, the two replicators then build two more in the next thousand seconds, the four build another four, and the eight build another eight. At the end of ten hours, there are not thirty-six new replicators, but over 68 billion. In less than a day, they would weigh a ton; in less than two days, they would outweigh the Earth; in another four hours, they would exceed the mass of the Sun and all the planets combined — if the bottle of chemicals hadn't run dry long before.

The astounding property of nanotechnology, and its potential to replicate in astronomical numbers, has worried some critics, who fear that a runaway replicator might threaten the entire planet, in a catastrophe they call the "grey goo" scenario. Drexler, however, thinks that the runaway-replication threat is overstated; it can easily be controlled, he says, with built-in limits. Later in *Engines of Creation*, he details some of the industrial applications of nanotechnology, describing just what nanotechnology in action might look like. He envisages watching a rocket engine as it is "grown" from a nanotechno-logical "seed" in a vat filled with a milky fluid of replicators and assemblers. The final product, he envisages, will be "a seamless thing, gemlike. Its empty internal cells, patterned in arrays about a wavelength of light apart, have a side effect: like the pits on a laser disc they diffract light, producing a varied iridescence like that of a fire opal ... Tap it, and it rings like a bell of surprisingly high pitch for its size."

Nanotechnology is where biotechnology meets microengineering. After all, the human body is itself a miracle of sophisticated nanotechnology in action. There might well be a convergence of the two disciplines in the near future; bioengineers who construct complex enzymes and retroviruses are already working with nanotechnology by default. The only difference between bioengineers and nanotechnologists is that the former do not build their tiny "machines" from scratch, but rather harness parts of pre-existing "nanomachines" found in nature. It might well transpire that biotechnology will be an alternative route to nanotechnology. If viruses and cells can be teased to construct organic nanomachines from the "blueprints" bioengineers provided, nanotechnology could be achieved through the back door.

Ultimately, however, by whatever means it is achieved, nanotechnology might well provide the mythical singularity that the technofuturists have predicted, since our technological potential would increase exponentially with its arrival. Unfortunately, its economic effect may be catastrophic, given that nanotechnology might spell the end of all corporately owned means of production — industrial, commercial, perhaps even agricultural — because nanotechnology would give individual households the ability to manufacture all their needs. After the initial and potentially destabilizing asymmetry between nations with replicators and those without them, there will be no surplus value to base trade on, aside from weapons, which will probably not be accessible for home replication. The only property or value that could potentially be traded after "the singularity" might be intellectual property — pure cognitive innovation. This and a host of other, possibly unanticipated ramifications, must be well considered before implementation of any research program with the potential to produce a functional replicator.

Chapter 12

TRANSHUMAN PSYCHOLOGY: Identity and Media

MULTIPLE PERSONALITIES

One of Buddha's most famous sermons was contained in his response to the enigma of human identity. One evening, just after the sun had set, a disciple asked the Buddha to explain the riddle of human identity. The Buddha answered without words. He seized a length of rope and plunged one end into a fire. Then, when the end of the rope had ignited, he whirled the rope in a great circle over his head. In the darkness there was a glowing ring of fire.

This famous mute sermon was interpreted in Buddhist scriptures as follows: although we experience our "self" as a single, unique identity, that experience is an illusion; in actuality, we are like the ring of fire in the night sky. The glowing ring results from the end of the rope whirling through countless different positions, like the spokes of a wheel, even though we see the glow as continuous. Just as the ring of fire actually comprises many separate points of fire, so the unique, individual personality is made up of many sub-personalities. Each incremental position of the glowing end of the rope is like a component of our identity. We normally don't see the various personalities of the whirling rope that make up our identity; we see only the totality.

This ancient teaching is verified by modern scientists studying the brain and its relationship to consciousness. Marvin Minsky, a computer scientist from MIT, asserts in his book *The Society of Mind* that human identity, our consciousness, is a hierarchy of thousands upon thousands of sub-routines, all unconscious of themselves, that add up to what we experience as awareness. His "society of mind" is like the various positions of the rope that make up the ring we call "self."

However, some of the sub-routines towards the very top of identity, just below conscious functioning, seem to be autonomous beings, identities in and of themselves. These sub-selves are often what psychologists call "personae," although some neurologists now argue that these sub-selves constitute a pre-integrated level of identity. This is why multiple-personality disorder is a very hot area in neurocognitive research, which speculates that victims of multiple-personality disorder are not suffering from a psychologically induced syndrome (even though they are portrayed as such in folk psychology and films like *The Three Faces of Eve*); rather, they are simply people whose various personalities are not fully integrated, whose ring of fire has disarticulated into its spokes. It could be said that we all possess the potential to have multiple-personality disorder, but we successfully sublimate our various personalities and meld them into one unified identity.

Cognitive technologies, such as computers and video games, will increasingly influence our identity. It is possible that singular, strong identities will no longer have the same viability they had in literate and industrial times. In fact, with the arrival of the transhuman era, rigidly inflexible single personalities may become a downright handicap. Human history has been moving towards this goal for hundreds of years.

Cosmopolitanism is a sign of our yearning to expand our personal repertoire of identities with new cultures and languages. Our ability to acquire new identity components from others is most efficient when we absorb the mannerisms and habits of people we admire, either family or friends. These character traits are as vital and deeply embedded in our memetic repertoire as our genetic inheritance is in our instinctual behaviour (although our personal inventory of models has ballooned recently under the influence of new media). Films and television are a particularly rich source of models, and our exposure to identity alternatives has increased a hundredfold in this century. World culture has also provided a plethora of cultural models to assimilate, via electronic media. As a result, some observers say, we risk suffering from identity-acquisition overload. However, as primates our natural ability for mimicry means we can adapt personae almost as quickly as we need them. Besides, over time we produce a series of personae — we are often not the same person we were a decade earlier. Our transformational proclivity feeds directly into the teratological and mutative effects of technology.

CD-ROM GAMES AND THE UNCONSCIOUS

Most of us have had dreams in which we are trying to run but our legs seem stuck in molasses. Objects seem to fall more slowly in dreams than they do in waking reality. It's as if the physical laws of dreams are of another order altogether. The dream medium seems slightly viscous and has some of the properties of both air and water. Also there is an ambiguous, unfinished quality to the dream's visual surroundings — upon waking it is hard to recollect specific details of a dream's background features. Oneiric narratives tend to unfold according to the dreamer's path through specific locales. (I call these locales "narrative shells" because each of them has its own mood and influence on a dream's narrative.) For example, in recurrent landscape dreams, dreamers often report having different experiences on different nights in the same dream landscape.

All of these qualities — slower-than-normal reactions, ambiguously detailed environments and narrative shells — are found in CD-ROM games such as Myst, Riven and Doom. Their uncanny simulation of the unconscious mind lends these games their spooky and unsettling feeling. It is possible that these qualities may have more to do with the temporary effects of transitional technologies than with anything else. But, if not, then it might transpire that computer games and some video games will become alternative points of entry into the unconscious which may, in turn, be able to provide us with a ready-made source of alternative identities in our forthcoming quest for multiple selves.

BEING OF TWO MINDS

Who can truthfully say he doesn't hold contrary beliefs? We claim not to be superstitious, and yet privately throw salt over our shoulders or avoid walking under ladders; we dislike a certain tune, and yet find ourselves mindlessly humming it. Rather than being evidence of the breakdown of logic, or of low-grade hypocrisy, our ability to hold contrary opinions, to be of "two minds," is really a practical solution to the difficulties of dealing with complex environments. It is a mark of our flexibility and evidence of our multiplicity that we accept new ideas without evicting our old "tenants."

The logical inconsistencies, the moral contradictions that most of us hold, are well within the normal range of a continuum that includes multiple-personality disorder at its farthest extreme. Whatever dramas we play out in our fantasies and regrets — the ones that start "If only I'd …" or "Maybe if I had …" — are understudied by one of our multiple personalities. (The actor's skill is really a bold step backwards and inwards.) We tend to invent identities and characters in order to act out a particular narrative, and then, if we take our lives elsewhere, these characters become forgotten identities that we allow to wither.

AUTOMOBILES, BODIES AND MINDS

A machine is a nexus of inventions and a metaphor for multiple identities. Most complex machines are colonies of smaller machines, the automobile being a good example. The engine, drive shaft and wheels are the central host that supports a group of "parasitic" systems whose functions are not necessary for propulsion; they include entertainment systems, climate control, gauges and window-servos.

An automobile is also a mosaic of individual tools. It is a composite entity made up of the commensal relations of its parts, that is, wheels attached to a chassis containing chairs. Separated from the car, these inner tubes, windows, springs, dials and batteries have independent, stand-alone applications. The wheel will roll by itself. Wheels and frame form a wagon that can be pulled by a horse. The interior of an abandoned car can act as a shelter.

Cars are industrial archaeologies. Their constituent parts recapitulate the various stages of technological evolution. In the historical stratification of any machine, each component is marked by its origin — be it iron age, industrial age or electronic age. The human body is a similar evolutionary aggregate. It has been suggested that some of our internal organs might originally have been commensal organisms whose became inextricably intertwined with our own. Regardless of the truth of this theory, it creates a useful metaphor for thinking about the body. Like cars, our bodies can be viewed as a composite system of stand-alone components that are themselves aggregates of cells, and so on, down to microscopic levels. The body is an array of semi-autonomous organs and functions that form an approximate, though functional, association.

It might be useful to understand our consciousness in the same light. We are, after all, aggregate consciousnesses, composed of ideas, concepts and attitudes borrowed from others. And, as Marvin Minsky has pointed out, the conscious mind is also an aggregate of hundreds of "delegated" functions that are co-ordinated by a centre of gravity we call "consciousness." The multiple-personality basis of our consciousness is reflected in its material basis also. The transhuman condition might well become a retrieval and elaboration of that multiplicity.

DIRT

For most of us, dirt is more an idea than a reality. I don't mean to say dirt is not real — our clothes do get soiled, and our floors do gather dust — but, specifically speaking, dirt's real composition is nebulous because it exists, for the most part, on a scale that requires magnification for it to be visible. For this reason, dirt is an excellent repository for peculiar suppositions about its constituents. Dirt's ambiguity attracts notions of contamination and anxiety. Dirt is contrary to intellectual consciousness. We like to be able to see the border and outlines of things around us. Dirt makes things fuzzy, unclear.

Dirt is really only dis-intactness, the little bits, the constituents of matter that are continually breaking off and falling away. From one point of view, the world is made of pre-dirt. That is why cleaning is a two-dimensional process. Only intact *surfaces* can be cleaned, although even they break off in very small quantities themselves. True "cleanliness" is possible only in ideal reality. Cleanliness is also highly relative. It is only a degree of fragmentation that spans the continuum that stretches from clean/shiny/new/intact through to broken/partially intact, and finally ends at fragmented/powdered.

Dirt represents entropy and decay. It is evidence of violated intactness. But our insistence on order is illusory, as all order is temporary intactness, and intactness itself is only a provisional state, an ideal condition. Even our bodies know this. Evolution has made us approximate organisms. As a result, debris in our food doesn't matter; our bodies can incorporate a certain amount of dirt without it affecting our consciousness or performance.

Freeman J. Dyson, in his book *Infinite in All Directions*, talks about "junk" in a sense that is not too far from the concept of "dirt":

> One of the most interesting developments in modern genetics is the discovery of "Junk DNA," a substantial component of our cellular inheritance which appears to have no biological function ... It is difficult to measure the fraction of our DNA that is functional. Several lines of evidence indicate that as much as half of it may be junk. The prevalence of Junk DNA is a striking example of the sloppiness which life has always embodied in one form or another. It is easy to find in human culture the analogue of Junk DNA. Junk culture is replicated together with genes. Junk culture is the rubbish of civilization, television commercials and jukeboxes and political propaganda. Tolerance of junk is one of life's most essential characteristics. In every sphere of life, whether cultural, economic, ecological or cellular, the systems which survive best are those which are not too fine-tuned to carry a large load of junk. And so, I believe, it must have been at the beginning. I would be surprised if the first living cell were not at least 25 percent junk.

ELECTRIC ANDROGYNY: A PSYCHOLOGY OF GENDER AND TECHNOLOGY

Gender Identity and Sexual Pleasure

Truly exquisite heterosexual lovemaking requires that the lovers are totally permeable to each other's androgyny. Each partner consists of male and female personae, and these personae spontaneously ebb and wax during lovemaking. It is therefore essential for the man to become empathetically female, from the inside out, in order to correctly pleasure the woman, as the woman must at times be able to adopt male sexuality. (These roles will be amplified by new technologies as they retrieve our multiple selves.) Blending into the partner's sexuality enables true empathy; it transcends all notions of self-centred satisfaction and "performance," whereas self-conscious performance turns making love into an impersonal travesty, really a kind of pornography between consenting partners.

At the same time, erotic love is about projected narcissism. The self is loved sufficiently by the self to be perfectly worthy of the beloved other. Sex, then, becomes a delicious, titillating form of self-arousal through the perfect medium of the other. Genitals become shared property — the closer the couple, the more their sex comes to approximate divine, mutual masturbation. It is here, in this intimate theatre, that we have enlisted the media to reflect, celebrate and augment the pleasure of lovemaking. Our willingness to admit the media belies our profound acceptance of their role.

Gender Appropriation and Transmigration

> *Women are female impersonators.*
>
> — Barbara Gowdy

Cross-dressing is gender appropriation. In terms of gender politics, male transsexuals are the ultimate expression of heterosexual male fetishism in that they possess the woman from the inside out. The male transsexual morphs into his ideal woman so that he can permanently enact the perennial male fantasy of "having" a beautiful woman's body for a day — to masturbate and to feel her breasts whenever the whim strikes him. Female impersonators and transsexuals are like ingenious stalkers who become their own lovers.

In terms of transhuman mutagenesis, however, transsexuals are prescient. Transvestites and transsexuals are *de facto* body-swappers. Their sexually motivated transmigration rehearses the physical transmigration that biotechnology will eventually make possible for us. That is why, increasingly, androgyny and sexual ambiguity, both in the media and in the streets, is becoming commonplace. Gender identity is the first, and most natural, place to start as we begin our transhuman mutagenesis.

Gender drift has been quietly gaining momentum since the late sixties with the "unisex" look, which was the direct result of the hippies' androgynous sexual ambiguity. The hermaphroditic sexuality of the sixties demonstrated equality of the sexes and initiated the drift of gender identity, and this drift was fortified in the seventies with the overt bisexuality of "Glam Rock." By the eighties, Boy George and Madonna introduced gay lifestyles into the mainstream, and the way was paved for the nineties fascination with "Voguing" and Ru Paul. Transsexuals are a natural premonitive symptom of the transhuman age.

Sexuality will likely expand from the present level of androgyny into a more elaborate, polymorphous eroticism. As well as gender ambiguity, hyper-genitalia will likely become a trend, and bioengineered sex organs might also become common — double genitals, perhaps; specialized functional modifications of the genitals, including size enhancements; as well as a greater degree of sensation achieved by creating more nerve endings in the sex organs. Transhumans and posthumans will not have to sacrifice any of their ancestral pleasures; if anything, they will elaborate and build on ones already in place as well as creating new ones.

OPEN FOR BUSINESS DURING RENOVATIONS: THE ONGOING NATURE OF TRANSITIONAL TECHNOLOGIES

The transhuman condition is liminal. We are constantly passing over thresholds in our perpetual state of transition through successive technologies. It seems that almost everything is simultaneously under construction and in use. The world of culture and technology has become a work-in-progress. We begin using our computers, faxes, cell phones and Internet browsers as soon as we get them. We read the manuals afterwards, if at all, because we don't have the time to learn all the rules, trading incomplete knowledge for experience in the social worlds opened up by our new technologies. We are too busy navigating these worlds to bother with anything more complicated than on/off switches and basic steering. And since we know that the operating skills of transitional technologies will be obsolescent in a few years anyway, we have a tendency to memorize only what we need to.

On another level, we are accustomed to being works-in-progress ourselves. We upgrade our consciousness with new information, new modalities and strategies, while still using older ones in order to keep functioning. As long as we live, the process of learning never stops, and if learning involves enlarging consciousness, then we are always in the state of renovation. Improvising solutions out of expediency is the essence of our existence. In that sense, transitional technologies mirror our natural state of being.

Chapter 13

JUMPING SHIP:
The Posthuman Era

IMMORTALITY

Life has used various strategies to ensure its survival over the ages; of these, sexual procreation is a relatively recent gambit. By far the greatest period of life's evolution, the first billion years, was spent as single-celled organisms that simply divided in order to reproduce themselves. With such asexual reproduction, there were no individuals, only "daughter" cells, which, if we regard them as a perpetuation of the original cell, led to functional immortality. It wasn't until later, at the level of complex, multicellular life forms, that life began to use sex and death as strategies of survival.

The paradox of human life is that we have become so complex that we are self-conscious. We have evolved into individual microcosms of the life drive. Consequently, our deaths cheat us out of our original goal, the drive to immortality that all life aspires towards. This paradox — the death of a self-aware life form that embodies the immortal aspirations of life — is a deep component of most religions.

We know that immortality is the rightful inheritance of self-consciousness, yet we also know that we are organic beings destined to die and never be again. This incompleteness, a temporary stage in our evolution, is about to be redressed. It is possible than the next few generations of humans will be among the last to die, and, if this is the case, future humans will regard the tragedy of death as an inconceivable horror and a cosmic waste. Aside from possible overpopulation the only challenge that these posthumans will face will be the awesome, perhaps frightening, prospect of eternal existence. Then again, immortality may not be as existentially intimidating as it appears to us now — continuous self-transformation and an endless supply of new experiences might well compensate for the metaphysical paradox of virtual immortality. What's more, the future configuration of consciousness may be so different from our present, individual consciousness that the entire dilemma of perpetual selfhood will be transcended.

UPLOADING CONSCIOUSNESS

The idea of "uploading" consciousness into a computer once struck me as a ludicrous notion: I knew, or at least I presumed to know, that the magnificent complexity of the human brain made any simplistic fantasy of simulating it in a computer laughably absurd. The brain contains ten-to-the-eleventh-power neurons alone. If you factor in that each neuron has roughly 36,000 connections, you can see why it seems beyond our capability to understand it, let alone upload its patterns. It wasn't until I read Daniel C. Dennett's *Consciousness Explained* that I realized that consciousness might be a much simpler trick than has been generally assumed. In the following passage, Dennett explains his view of human consciousness:

> Human consciousness is *itself* a huge complex of memes (or more exactly, meme-effects in brains) that can best be understood as the operation of a "*von Neumannesque*" virtual machine *implemented* in the *parallel architecture* of a brain that was not designed for any such activities. The powers of this *virtual machine* vastly enhance the underlying powers of the organic *hardware* on which it runs, but at the same time many of its most curious features, and especially its limitations, can be explained as the byproducts of the *kludges* that make possible this curious but effective reuse of an existing organ for novel purposes.

Although Dennett wasn't ostensibly making a pitch in his book for the possibility of uploading human consciousness into a computer, he certainly removed a lot of the conceptual barriers to that possibility. It is an easy jump from his statement to the consideration that human consciousness might be more easily coaxed out of our bodies than we had thought.

It was when I read *Mind Children*, by Hans Moravec, the director of the Mobile Robot Facility at Carnegie Mellon University, that I first began to take the idea of uploading more seriously. Here was a credible scientist who believed that there were no insurmountable scientific obstacles to eventually transferring human consciousness into a suitably complex receptacle. Because all bodily perceptions and functions could be simulated by the computer, and transferred into a waiting robot proxy, Moravec envisaged that the transition from flesh to silicon would be neither traumatic nor impossible.

UPGRADING CONSCIOUSNESS

There are many compelling reasons for humans to attempt this transition. One of them might be, as Dennett suggests, that the program of human consciousness is run imperfectly on our present biological substrate, that is, the human brain. His idea goes well beyond the folk notion that we use only a fraction of our minds at any time; rather, it addresses our deep impatience with the discrepancy between ideal, unhampered thought and the level of thinking we actually attain with our "provisional" biological equipment. Why are wisdom and knowledge so hard won? Who hasn't had the frustration of trying to think more clearly, or faster? Who hasn't wanted sharper and deeper memory? Not that our biological heritage hasn't served us well, but we know from whatever few flashes of effortless thought we have experienced in our lives that there is something better. We also know that the beauty, speed and mathematical elegance of effortless thought is our destiny. We see it in angels and utopias.

JUMPING SHIP: THREE MODELS

There are three likely scenarios for how human consciousness will first be transferred into a "machine." The first model, my personal favourite, is the gradual-replacement theory. It proposes that neural implants, inserted into the brain to assist mental functions, will eventually represent more than 50 percent of the brain. This process will be incremental, occurring over a long period of time, and we won't notice the "exact moment" when the brain has been uploaded. The second model, as Hans Moravec details below, is the direct, traumatic uploading of consciousness into a computer. The body is abandoned, to be replaced either by a synthetic body or by a simulated body in the computer. (A body of some sort would be necessary to satisfy the strong atavistic need — which may linger on through the divide — for a physical body.)

In his book *Mind Children*, Hans Moravec describes how the second model, uploading directly into a waiting computer, might be effected. He portrays how a highly specialized robot surgeon, using an array of microscopic tools, opens the client's skull and begins to analyse, simulate, and then bypass the original tissue. Once this bypass is complete, the brain is removed, layer by layer, neuron by neuron. Moravec then suggests an ingenious method of reassuring the client whose mind is being uploaded. This technique involves having the patient/client test the accuracy of the simulation (of a selected portion of his brain) by having a button at his fingertips that would alternate between the computer simulation and his original tissue, first by blocking impulses from the brain region being simulated and then by reverting back to the original tissue. In this way any discrepancies could be ironed out to the complete satisfaction of the client/patient.

When the client was assured that a particular section of brain function had been successfully simulated, then the simulation would take over permanently and the now-redundant section of brain tissue would be aspirated away. The process would be repeated for each section of brain until a simulation of the entire brain pattern would reside in the computer. Moravec then goes on to describe the final stage.

> Eventually your skull is empty, and the surgeon's hand rests deep in your brainstem. Though you have not lost consciousness, or even your train of thought, your mind has been removed from the brain and transferred to a machine. In a final, disorienting step the surgeon lifts out his hand. Your suddenly abandoned body goes into spasms and dies. For a moment you experience only quiet and dark. Then, once again, you can open your eyes. Your perspective has shifted. The computer simulation has been disconnected from the cable leading to the surgeon's hand and reconnected to a shiny new body of the style, color, and material of your choice. Your metamorphosis is complete.

It is important to realize that Hans Moravec believes that uploading human consciousness is scientifically feasible. He is quite serious. A third model, a science fiction version of another uploading procedure that stands halfway between Moravec's description and the gradual-replacement model, is sketched out in Greg Egan's book *Axiomatic.* In his fictional version of uploading, an instrument called the "Ndoli Device," implanted at birth, "learns" to simulate the mind perfectly.

Unlike many of my friends, I had no qualms whatsoever when, at the age of eighteen, the time came for me to "switch." My organic brain was removed and discarded, and control of my body handed over to my "jewel" — the Ndoli Device, a neural net computer implanted shortly after birth, which had since learnt to imitate my brain, down to the level of individual neurons. I had no qualms, not because I was at all convinced that the jewel and the brain experienced consciousness identically, but because, from an early age, I'd identified myself solely with my jewel. My brain was a kind of bootstrap device, nothing more, and to mourn its loss would have been as absurd as mourning my emergence from some primitive stage of embryological neural development.

Some Caveats

The basic dilemma posed by the possibility of extracting consciousness from the body, aside from its more-than-passing resemblance to the philosophical doctrine of vitalism, is closely related to neurology's search for the "seat of consciousness." This search has occupied cognitive science for more than a century. It devolves upon the question of which brain structures are precisely responsible for consciousness. This question remains to be answered (even though Dennett believes the question itself to be the problem), and the relationship between physical embodiment and consciousness might still turn out to be one of inextricability. We must then ask ourselves, if our body is so intimately intertwined with our consciousness, and if we attempted to upload our minds, then wouldn't traumatic death occur anyway, as a result of being in such an extreme state? Perhaps disembodiment would bring with it such unimaginable anguish that we would be able to maintain consciousness for only a brief time before dying of shock.

At this time we cannot know if we are dependent upon embodiment or not. Disembodied consciousness might be insufficient to maintain sanity. Or it might be a liberation of sorts, as Dennett seems to imply, and we will fly further and faster on our wings of thought than we had ever dreamed possible. We may well find out.

The Psychology of Uploaded Consciousness

One aspect of uploaded consciousness, if it is ever achieved, will be its transparency to observation. Uploaded consciousness might be an optimal site for the isolation and treatment of mental disorders, from schizophrenia to manic depression, not to mention neuroses. Certainly the accessibility of algorithmically encoded and digitized consciousness will allow for extraordinarily detailed observations of the linkages that underlay such pathologies. Perhaps the psychiatrists of the future will be computer programmers, or hackers, who break the codes of mental disorders and smooth out the irregularities and suffering of those who would otherwise have languished beyond therapeutic reach, in their organic state.

It might also transpire that the analyses done of uploaded consciousnesses will create a systematic natural history, a classification system of mental disorders that would have triggered Freud's envy. This would necessitate, among other things, a hugely complex three-dimensional, real-time map of brain function on a molecular level. The knowledge thus acquired could then be applied retroactively, with considerable clinical efficacy, to individuals who had not been uploaded.

At the same time, we mustn't forget that computers are extensions of our minds, and therefore, ultimately, of our psychologies. As our computers begin to mirror our consciousness, they will come to reflect our emotional states as well. Just as current computers suffer from viruses, it might not be unthinkable in the future for more sophisticated computers to suffer from human neuroses.

Some Additional Caveats

Before we jump on the digital gurney, there are still a lot of unanswered questions about human consciousness that have to be examined. There are major problems with the "brain as computer" metaphor. For example, liquids, with their non-linear flow, are very hard to quantify, and the brain is saturated with them. Do the hormones and neurochemicals that wash through our cortexes introduce randomness as a strategy of thought? Do neurohormones maintain the plastic flexibility of the cortex so necessary for learning? A cortex lacking these drifting modulators might simply lose the ability to break patterns and reroute signals. It might become functionlessly repetitive. An uploaded consciousness might be susceptible to unanticipated disorders of thought, like cognitive Parkinson's disease, suffering involuntary sequences of thoughts and utterances. All of these uncertainties will have to be overcome before a truly workable model for uploaded consciousness is even plausible.

There are certain intricacies of consciousness that further complicate the concept of uploading, at least in Moravec's scenario. For instance, is language an arbitrary, substitutional system, or is it completely dependent on its biological origin? This question has some bearing on the uploading issue because language has always been at the heart of human consciousness.

Some of the figure/ground relationships between language and awareness have been sketched out by philosophers. It is important, for example, that the problems of "engaged agents" as proposed by Wittgenstein and Heidegger are resolved, as they have great bearing on the codability of consciousness. Is meaning dependent on context, as Wittgenstein maintained? It would be a mistake to naïvely assume that consciousness was immune to dependency on the biological context and that the ostensive illusions of language blinded us to subtle complications in the transference of consciousness.

Cybermorphs as Uploading Receptacles and Familiars

If cybermorphs, the manipulatable figures we use to represent ourselves in cyberspace, achieve sufficient sophistication, they might become virtual receptacles for uploaded consciousness. Providing hardware receptacles for uploaded beings will then lose its priority. It might well transpire that the race for sufficient complexity will be between biotechnology and virtual (artificial) biology.

On the other hand, if biotechnology and robotics surpass virtual biology, then the physical forms that we use may be modelled on our personal cybermorphs and avatars. But, even if we embody our self-designed cyber-bodies, the fact that they are relatively fixed and static (because they exist as material objects) may make them too immobile and unchangeable to satisfy posthumans used to being able to transform into many different shapes and forms.

As did the fabled sorcerers of old, individual posthumans might have many cybermorphic shapes, like witches' familiars, some of which might well be animals. The whole world of mythology, already nascent in video games and television shows like "Hercules," might re-emerge in the cyber-realm as an index of identities mapped over the complex, manipulatable data and information of cyberspace. Even now, three-dimensional worlds filled with grotesque and fantastic cybermorphs are starting to convene at multiple-user sites on the Web.

POSTHUMAN ECONOMIES

The Commodification of Consciousness

Although full uploading of consciousness may prove to be a distant, or even impossible, goal, neural implants and perceptual amplification devices are relatively closer to practical application.

It takes no great leap of imagination to realize that, if consciousness should, ultimately, prove to be uploadable, corporations will hold patents on the software that will embrace our minds. We may, in the future, be able to realize an aphorism that is now only an allegory, by being able to literally sell our souls to a corporation. It may turn out that there will be a single corporate monopoly on the uploading technology and other cognitive technologies. It may also turn out that governments will have to intercede with legislation to ensure that platforms for consciousness are licensed (the way they have interceded in Canada in the marketing of generic drugs), forcing rival corporations to compete as they develop unique software and hardware for cognitive technologies. Alternatively, various companies might specialize in simulating various components of the brain, some concentrating in temporal-lobe simulations, others in cerebellums, and so on.

Composite Entities

Still, it remains possible that part of the transhuman's or posthuman's personal identity will bear the unique signature of a neural-prosthesis manufacturer. Furthermore, if sections of cognitive function are apportioned, with various companies specializing in specific parts of the brain, it might become possible for recipient individuals to acquire copyrighted living simulations of a portion of a gifted individual's brain, as licensed by the manufacturer. The well-heeled posthuman could acquire, say, the right-temporal-lobe simulation of a famous musician (with its personal memories erased) and the left-temporal-lobe simulation of a prominent writer (also with its personal memories erased).

On the other hand, becoming, even partially, a corporate cognitive product may be an identity threshold that humans will not wish to cross. After all, our current, private and mysteriously concocted consciousness is beyond ownership, both by evolutionary origin and by its creation. Nothing is purchased to create a human being in his or her current organic incarnation. We are, at present at least, not cognitive commodities.

Cognitive-Prosthesis Advertising

Our biological resistance to the commodification of identity will probably change in the posthuman era. Not only will the corporation's identity become an intrinsic part of personal identity, but all kinds of human skills, perceptions, memories and experiences might also become marketable in the ultimate intellectual-properties marketplace. If indefinite postponement of personal death includes the abandonment of our ageing bodies, we will make the bargain, but it's possible that we must prepare to have ourselves used for extraordinarily intimate endorsement advertising, particularly if we accomplish anything notable using our cognitive prosthesis.

Human beings are not aware of the physical "lower-level" unconscious functions — sub-programs such as the activities of the hypothalamus — that provide us with our conscious experience. We will remain unaware of them in the transhuman and posthuman eras, but it is possible that such discrete mental functions may, as I have mentioned earlier, be delegated to various servers. Thus, not only will substrate corporations be able to claim some authorial entitlement to our productions, they will also be able to advertise unconscious sub-routines of cognition and emotional simulations that, normally, we would be completely unaware of. Furthermore, if this is the case, they will likely have contracts with clauses covering this type of promotion, should we sign over our "substrate contract" in order to use their particular prosthesis. Imagine an advertising brochure of a cognitive-prosthesis corporation with the following voiceover and a corresponding 3D virtual presentation with colourful graphics and charts; "Our hypothalamic simulations are second to none. Here is a sequence of peak excitation in one of our clients during a re-enacted traumatic dream sequence. Notice the afferent spike-flattening on all of the post-hypothalamic junctions."

Corporate Control of Consciousness

The spectre of a corporate monopoly over posthuman consciousness is, clearly, nightmarish. Free and open markets, with multiple, evolving servers, are indispensable to the transhuman and posthuman economy. A highly competitive and selective marketplace driven by competition that grants maximum flexibility and freedom to the individual has to be maintained. Clients must be free to move from platform to platform as better cognitive services are offered, just as today we switch long-distance telephone carriers .

It should, however, be kept in mind that the preceding scenarios are contingent on the existence of individual transhuman and posthuman identities similar to our current ones. If there are radical changes to the nature of consciousness as a result of posthuman technology, it may well be that there will be no conflict among a corporate, computer or personal identity. The term "identity" may not even apply. Perhaps also, money, or any sort of monetary description of the exchange of data and energy, may be replaced by a series of transactions unrecognizable to today's economists.

Beyond Cybermorphs

The economy of posthuman capitalism will probably be based almost entirely on intellectual and information commodities. The vendors of cognitive services will compete for the "material" resources of the posthuman economy: computer processing time and memory storage space. The players in this market will be vastly more varied and heterogeneous than those in today's economy — they might include artificial entities, downloaded human consciousnesses, artificially enhanced posthuman individuals, and virtual corporations.

Transactions in the posthuman economy will be extraordinarily fast. Posthumans who compete with artificial intelligences will no longer be able to afford the luxury of aliases and avatars (cybermorphs) to represent them in their dealings. When we are forced to compete directly with algorithmic entities who have no such decorative baggage to hinder them, cybermorphs — as ironic and metaphorical as they are — will become relics that take up valuable storage space and computer processing time. Perpetuating such frivolous interfaces might well handicap posthuman competitors.

IDENTITY IN THE POSTHUMAN ERA

Species are collective entities — they produce multiple copies of themselves to ensure their survival. Although individuals within all species have unique character traits, human beings have taken uniqueness to its extreme with the deification of "individualism." In our meritocracy, we hold a special cultural reverence for the "individual genius," particularly in artistic endeavours. At the same time, in the democratic realm, we conversely insist on equal rights for all, regardless of an individual's uniqueness. In some respects, particularly with majority rule, it seems as if, with democracy, we have developed a political paradigm of species altruism, and our mass behaviours mirror the selective pressures of evolution — they have general results, not individual ones. Even with our contemporary liberal politics of graduated consensus, where the need to accommodate minorities counteracts the collective consensus, the leviathan of democracy will still not move for an individual. We presently embrace an implicit contradiction that might resolve itself politically in the transhuman era: our arts celebrate the unique, but our democratic politics extols the species.

With the fundamental redefinition of human consciousness will come radical repositioning in both culture and politics. It is a current assumption that the collective basis of our evolutionary biology has been transcended by our ideal of the unique individual, on the one hand, and by our political paradigm of species altruism, a sort of consensual virtual biology, on the other; however, the collective nature of posthuman consciousness may pre-empt the individual — at least, our current notions of individuality — entirely. It is not out of the question that the unique, individual human being is a transitional evolutionary stage, an ultimately expendable aberration that is now poised at the brink of a precipitous slide into collective consciousness. Individual human consciousness may well turn out to have been a temporary, but necessary, detour on the road to meta-consciousness.

The individual is uncanny, as self-consciousness is uncanny.

THE OMEGA POINT

We humans have reached the end of unassisted evolution. From now on, our development is in our hands. If we imagine for a moment that this same process has occurred elsewhere in the universe, then it is not improbable to imagine it having gone further. If, as Kevin Kelly suggests in his book *Out of Control*, we are destined for a "hive mind," then it seems statistically possible that some zenomorphs, light years away, have already become technical immortals who have transcended individuality and combined to form group beings of immeasurable power. The only barrier to these beings achieving actual immortality would be the finite nature of the universe and the immutable directionality of time. But even then, as Freeman J. Dyson pointed out in his book *Infinite in All Directions*, they could squeeze time out of entropy by using cooler temperatures to increase the speed of their computations. Perhaps these hypothetical zenomorphs could extend the duration of their lives by somehow reversing the direction of time, crossing back and forth from the end to the beginning of the universe. In either case, they would inevitably expand their control to incorporate every particle in the universe. Actually, that point of total incorporation, the "Omega Point," has already been postulated as the ultimate end point of human evolution by two cosmologists, Frank Tipler and John Barrow. In their landmark book, *The Anthropic Cosmological Principle*, they say that the Omega Point is where we will have "control of *all* matter and forces not only in a single universe, but in all universes whose existence is logically possible; life will have spread into *all* spatial regions in all universes which could logically exist, and will have stored an infinite amount of information, including *all* bits of knowledge which it is logically possible to know."

Humans, it seems, really are the material universe becoming conscious of itself. If we can extend our fantasy just a little further, it is precisely because of the Omega Point that the universe has to be finite. Perhaps the universe containing all possible universes can happen only once, and it must end because that is the only way to end the omnipotence of the eternal beings it will spawn.

Acknowledgements

I extend my gratitude and appreciation to my editor, Ed Carson, whose thematic reading of this book gave it its final shape. In addition I thank my partner, Barbara Gowdy, not only for her patience and support during the writing of the book, but also for her careful reading of the penultimate manuscript. As well, thanks go to my agent, Anne McDermid, for her dedication and professionalism. I'd also like to thank Brian Fawcett, for his attentive commentary on an early version of the manuscript.

Much thanks is due to those who assisted at HarperCollins. It was Iris Tupholme who first championed the book and who then guided it through all stages of preparation. I am also indebted to Nicole Langlois, Neil Erickson, Gordon Robertson, Richard Bingham and Christian Bailey for their expertise and enthusiasm.

During the writing of the book I received both intellectual and logistical support from Derrick deKerckhove, Derek Robinson, Bruce Powe, Darren Wershler-Henry and Wodeck Szemberg, and, in the final stages, from Evan Solomon and Jill Offman. Lastly, thanks to the Canada Council and the Ontario Arts Council.

Bibliography

Adams, Peter. *Moon, Mars and Meteorites*. Cambridge: Cambridge University Press, 1986.

Albers, R. Wayne, and George J. Siegel, Robert Katzman and Bernard W. Agranoff. *Basic Neurochemistry*. Boston: Little, Brown and Company, 1972.

Ballard, J.G. *Highrise*. London: Jonathan Cape, 1975.

Barrow, John D., and Frank J. Tipler. *The Anthropic Cosmological Principle*. London: Oxford University Press, 1988.

Barthes, Roland. Translated by Colin Smith and Anette Lavers. *Writing Degree Zero*. London: Jonathan Cape, 1967.

Bateson, Gregory. *Steps to an Ecology of Mind*. New York: Ballantine, 1972.

Becker, Ernest. *The Denial of Death*. New York: Macmillan, 1973.

Burroughs, William. *Nova Express*. New York: Grove Press, 1965.

Burroughs, William. *The Soft Machine*. New York: Grove Press, 1967.

Chomsky, Noam. *The Chomsky Reader*. New York: Pantheon Books, 1987.

Coupland, Douglas. *Microserfs*. Toronto: HarperCollins, 1995.

Dawkins, Richard. *The Selfish Gene*. London: Oxford University Press, 1976.

De Kerckhove, Derrick. *The Skin of Culture*. Toronto: Somerville House Publishing, 1995.

Dennet, Daniel. *Consciousness Explained*. Boston: Little, Brown and Company, 1991.

Dennet, Daniel. *Kinds of Minds*. New York: HarperCollins, 1996.

De Saussure, Ferdinand. *Course in General Linguistics*. New York: McGraw-Hill, 1996.

Dilson, Jesse. *Electronics*. Toronto: Crowell-Collier, 1962.

Drexler, K. Eric. *Engines of Creation*. New York: Anchor Books, 1986.

Dyson, Freeman. *Infinite in All Directions*. New York: Harper & Row, 1988.

Freud, Sigmund. Translated by A.A. Brill. *The Basic Writings of Sigmund Freud*. New York: Random House, 1938.

Freud, Sigmund. Translated by James Strachey. *Case Histories II*. New York: Pelican, 1979.

Freud, Sigmund. Translated by James Strachey. *Introductory Lectures on Psychoanalysis*. New York: W.W. Norton & Company, 1966.

Gibson, William. *Neuromancer*. New York: Ace Books, 1984.

Gleick, James. *Chaos: Making a New Science*. New York: Viking, 1987.

Gould, Stephen Jay. *Wonderful Life: The Burgess Shale and the Nature of History*. New York: W.W. Norton & Company, 1989.

Gregory, R.L. *Eye and Brain: The Psychology of Seeing*. New York: McGraw-Hill, 1966.

Hawking, Stephen W. *A Brief History of Time: From the Big Bang to Black Holes*. New York: Bantam Books, 1988.

Herr, Michael. *Dispatches*. New York: Alfred A. Knopf, 1977.

Hofstadter, Douglas R. *Gödel, Escher, Bach: An Eternal Golden Braid*. New York: Basic Books, 1979.

Jung, Carl G. Translated by R.F.C. Hull. *Dreams*. Princeton, NJ: Princeton University Press, 1974.

Kelly, Kevin. *Out of Control*. Reading, MA: Addison Wesley, 1994.

Lacan, Jacques. *The Language of Self*. New York: Delta, 1975.

Lakoff, George, and Mark Johnson. *Metaphors We Live By*. Chicago: The University of Chicago Press, 1980.

Lévi-Strauss, Claude. *The Savage Mind*. Chicago: The University of Chicago Press, 1966.

Lotringer, Sylvère. *Overexposed*. New York: Pantheon Books, 1988.

McGinn, Colin. *The Character of Mind*. London: Oxford University Press, 1982.

McLuhan, Marshall. *Understanding Media: The Extensions Of Man*. Toronto: McGraw Hill, 1964.

McLuhan, Marshall, and Eric McLuhan. *Laws of Media: The New Science*. Toronto: University of Toronto Press, 1988.

Miller, George A., and Elizabeth Lenneberg, eds. *Psychology and Biology of Language and Thought: Essays in Honor of Eric Lenneberg*. New York: Academic Press, 1978.

Minsky, Marvin. *The Society of Mind*. New York: Simon & Schuster, 1985.

Monod, Jacques. *Chance and Necessity*. New York: Random House, 1971.

Moravec, Hans. *Mind Children*. Cambridge, MA: Harvard University Press, 1988.

Nathan, Peter. *The Nervous System*. London: Oxford University Press, 1983.

Negroponte, Nicholas. *Being Digital.* New York: Alfred A. Knopf, 1995.

Nietzsche, Friedrich. Translated by Thomas Common. *The Philosophy of Nietzsche.* New York: Random House, 1954.

Nietzsche, Friedrich. Translated by Walter Kaufman. *The Gay Science.* New York: Random House, 1974.

Nietzsche, Friedrich. Translated by Walter Kaufmann. *Thus Spake Zarathustra.* New York: Viking, 1954.

Oatley, Keith. *Brain Mechanisms and Mind.* London: Thames and Hudson, 1972.

Pagels, Heinz R. *Perfect Symmetry.* New York: Simon & Schuster, 1985.

Popper, Karl R., and John C. Eccles. *The Self and Its Brain.* Berlin: Springer International, 1981.

Regis, Ed. *Great Mambo Chicken and the Transhuman Condition.* Reading, MA: Addison Wesley, 1990.

Roazen, Paul. *Freud and his Followers.* New York: New York University Press, 1984.

Rucker, Rudy. *Software.* New York: Avon Books, 1987.

Rucker, Rudy. *Wetware.* New York: Avon Books, 1988.

Russell, Bertrand. *A History of Western Philosophy.* London: Unwin Hyman, 1946.

Ryle, Gilbert. *The Concept of Mind.* New York: Hutchinson, 1949.

Sacks, Oliver. *The Man Who Mistook His Wife for a Hat: and Other Clinical Tales.* New York: Summit Books, 1985.

Saul, John Ralston. *The Unconscious Civilization.* Toronto: Anansi, 1995.

Shannon, Claude E. *The Mathematical Theory of Communication.* Chicago: University of Illinois Press, 1964.

Smith, Robert J. *The Psychopath in Society*. New York: Academic Press, 1978.

Stapledon, Olaf. *Odd John*. New York: E.P. Dutton, 1936.

Stevens, Jay. *Storming Heaven: LSD and the American Dream*. New York: Harper & Row, 1987.

Thompson, D'Arcy [1917]. *On Growth and Form*. Cambridge: Cambridge University Press, 1961.

Turkle, Sherry. *Life on the Screen: Identity in the Age of the Internet*. New York: Simon & Schuster, 1995.

Virilio, Paul, and Sylvère Lotringer. *Pure War*. New York: Semiotext(e), 1983.

Whorf, Benjamin Lee. 1956. *Language, Thought and Reality*. Cambridge, MA: Massachussets Institute of Technology Press, 1956.

Wittgenstein, Ludwig. *Philosophical Investigations*. London: Oxford University Press, 1958.

Yates, Frances A. *The Art of Memory*. Chicago: University of Chicago Press, 1966.

Young, J.Z. *Programs of the Brain*. London: Oxford University Press, 1978.

Yurick, Sol. *Metatron*. New York: Semiotext(e), 1985.

Index

About the Author

Christopher Dewdney has published more than eleven volumes of poetry. He has also written several books about media, culture and human consciousness, subjects that continue to fascinate him. As well as being Academic Advisor at Calumet College, he teaches creative writing at York University. He is also a media and culture commentator and has appeared regularly on TVO's *Studio 2* among other television and radio programs. He has lived in Toronto for almost two decades and grows bamboo in his garden.